Restoring
Sexual Sanity

Restoring Sexual Sanity

RANDY C. ALCORN

FOREWORD BY D. JAMES KENNEDY, PH.D.

Unless otherwise indicated, Scripture quotations are from the Holy Bible: New International Version, @ 1973, 1978, 1984 by the International Bible Society. Used by permission of Zondervan Bible Publishers.

RESTORING SEXUAL SANITY

© 2000 by Randy C. Alcorn
Published by Coral Ridge Ministries
Ft. Lauderdale, FL 33308

Originally published as *Christians in the Wake of the Sexual Revolution: Recovering our Sexual Sanity* (Multnomah, 1985)

Printed in the United States of America

To Nanci,
whose loyal love
makes marriage a privilege
and a pleasure.

CONTENTS

Foreword
D. James Kennedy, Ph.D.

The Bible says, "Marriage is honorable among all, and the bed undefiled; but fornicators and adulterers God will judge" (Hebrews 13:4). From a Christian perspective, sex is holy in the context of marriage. Any deviation from that is wrong.

Of course, many today do not share this view of sexuality. They feel that as long as "there is love," then virtually anything is permissible. They feel as if, at long last, mankind has emerged out into the bright, warm sunshine of sexual freedom; man has been emancipated from the slavery of sexual taboos. It's as new as modern science, as fresh and sparkling as the rocket that carried our men to the moon. I remember once hearing a television discussion on sexual problems, marriage, divorce, etc. Several experts were being interviewed, and the question was asked, "Are there no moral standards anymore concerning sex?" One of the experts said, "No." That was accepted, without question. All the mores have gone by the board. We live in a new free society where anything goes. In my heart there cried out the words, "What about God?" Is God dead; does not the One who created us have the right to govern us? What about the moral commandments of God? It matters not how many millions of people conspire together to break the commandments of God. We can only break ourselves against them. God gives us time to repent before the Judgment comes, but it will invariably come. The moral commandments of God remain unchanged.

The Bible presents sex as holy within marriage alone, and even the thought life is to be holy. This ethic, therefore, condemns premarital sex (fornication), adultery, homosexuality, bestiality, incest, and pornography. These standards were given by the Creator of this universe, the Maker of man. We ignore these standards to our own temporal and eternal peril.

Satan has always been saying to mankind, "Do it my way and you're going to find fullness of life, enjoyment, satisfaction, fulfillment and joy." This is the way it always has been from the very beginning. Satan said, in effect, to Eve, "Don't listen to God. He is not with it! Why, He's got a narrow, mean view! He is going to make you miserable and frustrated! If you want to really swing, have a little bite on me and your eyes will be opened." That sounded good and so she took, she ate, she found shame, humiliation, guilt, sickness, and death instead. And there was much laughter as Satan promised there would be, but it was in Hell on the part of the demons. They continually deceive people in the same way down through the ages.

When God gave, for example, the commandment to not commit adultery, He was protecting the sanctity of sex. Immediately after giving the Commandment to protect the sacredness and sanctity of life itself, God moved to protect and guard the sanctity of the highest earthly relationship man can know—the relationship of the husband and wife. It was given to purify and protect the procreation of life. Since marriage is the most basic of all human relationships—from it all others, such as the Church, or the state, are built up—it is essential that marriage be jealously guarded from every form of attack. In our time, the institution of marriage is under severe siege.

The command is emphatic. It is simple, unqualified, irrevocable and negative: "Thou shalt not commit adultery." There is no argument annexed; there is no reason given. So destructive and pernicious and damning is the sin involved that none is needed. When Jesus came, He broadened the scope of this command. Not only was the act of adultery a sin, but now committing adultery in the heart was a sin. He says, "But I say to you that whoever looks at a woman to lust for her has already committed adultery with her in his heart" (Matthew 5:28). The lustful look is condemned—the sin of the heart; for it is out of the heart that there proceeds all manner of iniquity, and God calls us to guard our hearts and our minds.

It is said that unmarried people who remain chaste will experience all sorts of psychological trauma. People are told to satisfy all of their desires. One man told me that he had never kissed a woman until he kissed his fiancé. Another woman told me that she had frequent sexual liaisons with numerous people. You might readily conclude that the man was someone who had been locked up in a psychopathic ward somewhere, having broken down under the frustration of it all, and that the woman was evidently a prime example of the liberated woman with a healthy mind and body. Actually I met the woman in the psychiatric ward of a hospital, and the man is named Billy Graham.

Probably the basic lie of Satan underlying this in all of his deceptions is that the laws of God will restrict and narrow and diminish one's life. How many people have sadly learned that just the opposite is the truth, when their bodies have been vitiated by venereal disease, or their minds have been scrambled by various guilt-induced psychoses or neuroses, and found, only too late, that had they followed God's path, their life would have been enriched and ennobled?

The problem is that in America today we have confused love with lust, and these are almost antithetically opposed to one another. The essence of lust is a desire to get something from someone else. Love is the opposite. "For God so loved, He gave . . ." Love gives; lust takes.

It's time for the Church in America to wake up. That's why I'm excited to offer this book, an update of Randy Alcorn's classic *Christians in the Wake of the Sexual Revolution.* It provides an excellent diagnosis of how we got off track, and it gives clear answers on what we can do to help restore sexual sanity in our families, churches, and our country before it's too late.

—D. *James Kennedy, Ph.D.,*
Pastor of Coral Ridge Presbyterian Church,
Ft. Lauderdale, Florida

PREFACE

When I started writing this book, I envisioned a practical "how to" guide for resisting sexual temptation. Though I've written on that subject since,* this isn't that book.

The more I researched and evaluated, the more I became convinced that practical advice about sex must be built on a proper foundation of right thinking about sex. Without this foundation, the practical help can at best engender a superficial morality (superior to immorality, but far less than ideal).

My pastoral and counseling experience has demonstrated to me that the majority of believers simply do not have this moral foundation upon which to build. We may hear the right words, speak them, and profess to believe them, but the photographic plates of our minds have been exposed so long and so thoroughly to the world that the Word doesn't seem to sink in.

There is much wrong sexual behavior among Christians, to

*Sexual Temptation, Randy C. Alcorn (1996, Eternal Perspective Ministries, 2229 East Burnside #23, Gresham, OR 97030).

be sure, but *wrong thinking is at the root of the wrong behavior*. We've failed to identify this wrong thinking and its sources—and failed to eliminate or reject them. We've indiscriminately bought the antibiblical sexual propaganda foisted on us by the world, largely through the media. This always leads to more wrong thinking and, eventually, more wrong behavior. While I have included much that is practical in this book, I've sought to avoid the stopgap fallacy of telling people how to change their behavior without helping them change their thinking.

I am acutely aware there are many risks in tackling the subject matter of this book. If I handled it with delicately veiled references, it would have no impact. Yet by being specific in my illustrations, I run the risk of conjuring up images that present sexual temptations. I may also sometimes appear to be negative in a day when being negative is considered worse than being dishonest. I am consoled that the Bible itself is full of warnings and corrections. To ignore the negative is not only unbiblical and naive, it destines an author to irrelevance, since his readers live in a world that is painfully real.

While I emphasize the beauty of sex as God intended it, I also point out the ugliness of abusing God's gift of sex. Many of the subjects in this book are admittedly disturbing, but they cry out for our attention. Scripture says, "It is shameful even to mention what the disobedient do in secret" (Ephesians 5:12). Yet the previous verse tells us "Have nothing to do with the fruitless deeds of darkness, but rather expose them." How can you expose something if you refuse to talk about it?

The one justification for discussing immorality is to expose it for what it is; to condemn, curb, and prevent it—and motivate others to do the same. The Bible speaks clearly and directly about sexual immorality, not to entice us but to tutor us in the path of righteousness. I have tried to follow this example. The result is a book that will not always help you feel good, but will hopefully help you be good.

It might appear to some that I have hung out the Church's dirty laundry before the world. But what is the alternative? Silence? A pussyfooting approach that fails to address head-on what is threatening both the life and witness of the holy Church of Christ?

God's Word answers by example. It does not showcase spiritual giants or gloss over the vulnerabilities and failures of the saints. On the contrary, Scripture is painfully honest in describing flesh-and-blood men and women with whom the twenty-first century believer can readily identify. As this book falls into the hands of non-Christians and young Christians, I can only hope they will understand and respect the need for the Christian community to take hard stock of itself in an honest effort to shore up its sagging morality.

When I wrote the original version of this book fifteen years ago, it was before the notorious scandals involving prominent television evangelists and pastors. Because the church failed to clean up its own act, the world stepped in and exposed its immorality. We who should have been offering the world the alternative to its impurity instead appeared to be offering moral impotence and hypocrisy.

No illustrations in this book are fictitious, but I have gone to great lengths to protect the identities of people. Not only names, but some details are changed, though the essential factors that bear on each illustration have not been distorted.

I want to acknowledge my debt to the Lord Jesus, to whom I owe all and to whose glory this book is offered. Thanks and praise go to Nanci, my wife, and Karina and Angie, my daughters. Without their understanding and sacrifices, my efforts would have been impossible or worthless.

Thanks also to my assistant, Kathy Norquist, and the wonderful folks at Coral Ridge Ministries, who assisted in revising and updating this book.

Edmund Burke's classic observation kept me going when everything within me wanted to fold under the weight of this project: "All that is necessary for the triumph of evil is that good men do nothing." This book is an attempt to do something.

PART 1

Where Does the World End and the Church Begin?

CHAPTER 1

Sex, the World, and the Church

Ask the enlightened American what he thinks of Christian sexual morality. To him, it's a fossil—an antique that went out with washboards and penny candy. Who believes any more what the Bible says about sex? Old ladies and helpless traditionalists, the same quaint folk who still use push lawn mowers, typewriters, and clothes that are years out of style.

The moral ice-age is over. Exit the dogmatic dinosaurs of sexual repression. Enter the sensuous sirens of sexual expression. We live in the age of sexual enlightenment, presumably but a few years from sexual utopia. *So what does this bright new age look like?*

Newspapers publish invitations for sexual partners. A singing telegram service sends male strippers to act out sexual fantasies in private homes. Rows of pornographic tabloids line city streets, available to any child with a curious mind and a few

3

spare quarters. Prostitutes, massage parlors, adult book stores, strip joints, peep shows, female impersonators, gay baths, singles bars, sado-masochist leather shops—they've become as much a part of urban America as skyscrapers and parking meters.

"But that's just the big city." My church, believe it or not, is in Boring, Oregon (a town less eventful than its name). Yet a mile away from our church building a tavern features nude dancers. Want ads in a nearby community college's newspaper solicit homosexual partners. The convenience store down the road stocks a dozen pornographic magazines and a rack of porno novels.

There is open season on sex in this country, and you don't have to look far to see it.

Strolling Through the Sexual Wasteland

Walking through a new shopping mall, my wife and I stepped into a gift store where children were huddled around battery operated stuffed animals. Ten feet into the store we were surrounded by nude puzzles, sex games, sex gadgets, and sex potions. Family variety stores sell pin-up posters of celebrities in seductive poses, along with "Playmate," "Buns," and "Hunk-A-Month" calendars. Bumper stickers and license plate frames boast of the driver's sexual prowess ("Nurses do it. . ." "Carpenters do it . . .") and scorn traditional morality ("Chaste Makes Waste"). Teenage boys wear T-shirts reading "Sex Instructor—First Lesson Free" and teen girls "I am a virgin—this is an old T-shirt."

Stopping at a motel on a business trip, a man is asked "Do you want adult movies? Do you want a woman?" Driving through a city, we stopped near two junior high boys in shorts and tank tops. Next to us a Lincoln Continental drove up, and the male driver beckoned to the boys. "Which one of us do you want?" one of the boys asked. When the man pointed his finger, the other boy hopped into the car. Teen prostitution— a multimillion dollar business in America.

A few blocks from the Bible college I graduated from, there is a massage parlor located directly across from a grade school, in full view of the children. A mile up the street, across from a high school, is a topless soft drink bar where students can view nude dancing during lunch hour.

Incest is at epidemic proportions. Whether at day care centers or in prostitution-pornography rings, child molesting makes the papers virtually every week. So do rape, sodomy, and serial sex murders. Organized clubs of transvestites, sadomasochists, and pedophiles have joined homosexuals by coming out of the closet and actively lobbying for their rights.

The new technology has become the tool of this new morality. When I subscribed to a computer newsletter, I was offered software disks featuring nude women. Now, the Internet has become one of the biggest ways pornographers market their wares. One of those warning about this lucrative business is Donna Rice Hughes, who was once involved in the sexual scandal with presidential hopeful Gary Hart. Today she is a Christian and is fighting against pornography. She said recently that the pornography industry is at least the third largest money-maker in cyberspace, with 100,000 pornographic sites on the Internet.

Though I have never once gone to a pornographic site on my computer, I regularly receive unsolicited e-mails with links to sexually explicit web sites only a double click away. (Parents who allow their children unrestricted Internet access in the privacy of their own rooms are fooling themselves if they think they are not visiting these sites.)

I was invited to speak at a well-known Christian liberal arts college for a week on the subject of sexual purity. The reason? Students in the school library were routinely accessing pornographic websites in full view of others. When the administration tried to restrict access, there were outraged cries of "censorship."

Millions receive by mail color catalogues featuring sex paraphernalia, every variety of pornography, and women's intimate apparel catalogues that rival the *Playboy* magazines of a generation ago.

A local television news program featured a human interest story on a striptease performer. The slant was that strip bars create jobs, meet a public need, and cause no harm. The stripper interviewed was a bright, cheerful college student who makes good grades and considers stripping a "challenging profession."

A Classic Lesson from Miss America

Go back with me to 1984, when Miss America resigned after *Penthouse* magazine published ten pages of her nude photos, depicting sexual overtures to another nude woman. The whole scenario was an instructive lesson in modern morality.

Miss America practiced modern morality when she sought to promote her career and earn her money by posing nude, and again later when she signed a statement for the pageant saying she had never been involved in any "moral turpitude." The photographer followed the same code of ethics by lying to the girl ("no one will ever see them") and selling the photos to the highest bidder. *Penthouse* showed its true colors (as if there were ever a doubt) by publishing the photos, despite knowing they would humiliate the girl, force her to resign, and possibly ruin her career.

The Miss America Pageant demonstrated its own moral hypocrisy by uplifting "traditional virtues" in calling for the girl's resignation (a correct decision), despite the fact that the pageant's most celebrated event is the swimsuit competition, a form of sexual exploitation different only in degree, not in kind, from *Penthouse's*. The American media demonstrated its moral integrity by reveling over the whole affair for days on end, thereby supplying millions of dollars worth of free advertising for *Penthouse*.

Finally, the American public not only enjoyed soaking up the media's account of this sordid mess but committed its own moral turpitude by buying every one of the month's five million copies (the number of "readers" per magazine being far higher), thus rewarding the unprincipled for their immoral decisions and tactics and driving up the price the next time a photographer seeks to similarly exploit a not-so-innocent young woman. Here we see in miniature the supply and demand cycle of America's waning sexual morality.

In the subsequent years this woman has become a well-known actress, who acknowledges she was launched into fame through an incident that once would have ended a career rather than launching it. The White House sex scandals at the end of the '90s served as the obituary on moral standards in America. Many were largely unphased by the shock and disgrace felt by many in "developing countries," who could not believe America had sunk so low.

The Search for Sex—The New Holy Grail

Harper's Bazaar asks, "Can sex cure arthritis?" The question typifies our age. Surely, sex is the answer to everything.

Television, movies, radio, books, magazines, newspapers, and music all constantly bombard us with sex. Thousands of industries, from cameras to computers—most of which have about as much to do with sex as athletes have to do with rental cars—use sex to sell their products. Even the scientific journals seem preoccupied with sex. I saw an article on prehistoric sex and another on insect foreplay.

The American sexual hype borders on the pathological. Were a future civilization to one day unearth the telltale ruins of present-day America, it would undoubtedly conclude we spent a third of our time having sex, another third planning it, and the other third talking about it.

Our obsession with sex is so great that anyone who doesn't share it is considered abnormal. According to *Time*, sex therapists report that one half of their cases focus on the problem of Inhibited Sexual Desire (ISD). They estimate that 20 percent of the population suffers from ISD.

"The biggest surprise so far," says one psychotherapist and sex researcher, "is how well these people are functioning. They look good, feel happy, like their families and are successful in their work."[1] *So what's the problem?* Despite the happy appearance of ISD victims, the psychotherapist feels bound to add this ominous conjecture: "But under the cheerfulness there's a lack of fulfillment." The irony is that most of these people are coming for help (which includes being taught to fantasize about sex) only because their society has intimidated them into believing that eroticism is essential to personal worth and happiness. No one points out that unbridled sexual lust destroys countless more lives than does ISD.

Though the American Psychiatric Association removed homosexuality from its list of disorders in its diagnostic handbook, it added ISD. Apparently, any sex is better than no sex.

But is it possible that the sexual revolution itself has robbed people of their sexual desire—intimidated them into backing off from sex because they cannot perform by society's numbers? Among its sexually liberated readership, *Psychology Today* reports an "astonishing" 28 percent of men and 40 percent of women hold back from sexual intimacy "due to a lack of desire." It is a significant exposé of the sexual revolution that, according to this study, "among men, the largest proportion who lack desire (41%) have had at least seven extramarital affairs."[2] So much for the lie of liberation.

Sexual Health or Sexual Sickness?

The sexual revolution has fostered a barnyard morality that robs human dignity. It has resulted in people being seen and treated as sexual objects rather than sexual subjects. It has left us a nation of technological giants and moral dwarves. Millions now live under the burden of sexual expectations and pressures to perform in a prescribed manner. Victims of the tyranny of the orgasm, they feel that unless their sexual experience is what they see in the media—where everyone is effortlessly erotic and every encounter is comparable to nuclear fission—they're being robbed, or they're not a real man or a real woman.

Instead of a spontaneous expression of other-oriented marital love, sex has become a self-oriented, goal-oriented obsession—an object of endless analysis, comparison, experimentation, and disappointment. Like the end of the rainbow, the ultimate sexual experience is always sought, but never found. No matter how hard we try, no matter how much we pay to surgically alter our bodies, we are left pathetic creatures, different in degree but not in kind from burnt out prostitutes standing on street corners.

Our modern sexual openness is endlessly pawned off as healthy, emancipating, and long overdue. But is our preoccupation with sex really a sign of sexual health? Who talks most about how they're feeling? Sick people. Who buys the books on car repairs? Those with car problems. Who buys the drain cleaner? Those with clogged drains. Who thinks about, talks about, and buys the most books about sex? Those with sexual problems.

Notice how much of the literature on sex deals with sexual problems, inadequacy, impotence, and dysfunction. This betrays not just a strong interest in sex, but a prevailing difficulty with it. Why do we still need so much help with sex? After forty years of sexual freedom, where's the sexual utopia promised us in the sixties and seventies? It's not knowledge of sex we lack, but *perspective*.

The move from the famine of Victorianism to the feast of eroticism hasn't been what it was cracked up to be. Like people who have bought choice real estate that turns out to be swampland, we've bought a lie—and a costly one at that.

The more we say about sex, the more we herald the new liberating sexual doctrines, the more we seem to uncover (or is it produce?) a myriad of sexual problems. The harder we try to drown these sexual problems in a flood of new relationships, erotic magazines, novels, movies, and sex education literature and classes, the louder and more persistently our sexual problems cry out for attention. We have become little more than a nation of sexual misfits. An honest look at our newspapers, magazines, television programs, and a host of other social gauges substantiates this. The more we talk about sex and trump up sexual liberty, the more we forge the chains of our sexual slavery.

The more we have sought fulfillment apart from God, the further into the sexual desert we have wandered. Throats parched, lips cracked and bleeding, we are nomads in search of a sexual oasis that forever eludes us.

Galatians 6:7 says it perfectly: "Do not be deceived. God cannot be mocked. A man reaps what he sows."

We have turned our backs on the Architect, Engineer, and Builder of human sexuality. We have denied his authority and ridiculed his servants. Our glands as our gods, we have discarded his directions, burned his blueprint, trampled on the ashes, and, like rebellious children, stalked off to do sex our own way. And we are reaping the results.

How Different Is the Church?

In 1959 A. W. Tozer wrote,

> The period in which we now live may well go down in history as the Erotic Age. Sex love has been elevated into a cult. Eros has more worshippers among civilized men today than any other god. For millions the erotic has completely displaced the spiritual.[3]

Though he had harsh words for the effects of eros on the world, Tozer's concern was for something far more serious:

> Now if this god would let us Christians alone I for one would let his cult alone. The whole spongy, fetid mess will sink some day under its own weight and become excellent fuel for the fires of hell, a just recompense which is meet, and it becomes us to feel compassion for those who have

been caught in its tragic collapse. Tears and silence might be better than words if things were slightly otherwise than they are. But the cult of eros is seriously affecting the church. The pure religion of Christ that flows like a crystal river from the heart of God is being polluted by the unclean waters that trickle from behind the altars of abomination that appear on every high hill and under every green tree from New York to Los Angeles.[4]

If Tozer were still with us, he would be both grieved and outraged to discover the sad truth—that the Church's moral life in 1959 was *far* superior to what it is today. In New Testament times, the sexual purity of God's people drew a sharp line dividing them from the non-Christian world. Prior to the sexual revolution, this was largely true of the Church in America. But things have radically changed. In *Flirting with the World*, John White draws these sobering conclusions: "the sexual behavior of Christians has reached the point of being indistinguishable from that of non-Christians . . . in our sexual behavior we, as a Christian community, are both in the world, and of it."[5]

Christians in Moral Crisis

Substantiating White's claim was this paradox uncovered by a 1984 Gallup poll sixteen years ago: "Religion is growing in importance among Americans, but morality is losing ground." That same poll found "very little difference in the behavior of the churched and unchurched on a wide range of items including lying, cheating, and pilferage."[6] In the years since the distinction between world and Church has continued to fade.

High standards of morality—including sexual morality—used to be inseparable from the Christian faith. No longer. It is increasingly difficult to discern where the world ends and the Church begins.

Examples are not hard to come by.

Christians and the Media

My observations and conversations confirm there is little difference between the media habits of Christians and those of their non-Christian neighbors. There are those who feel the freedom to frequently miss church but would never miss the latest drama or sitcom that is filled with sexual depictions, references and innuendos. We are hopelessly naive to think that Christians do not watch such programs—or that watching them we are somehow immune to their effects.

A Christian couple confided they subscribe to an adult entertainment network that brought X-rated movies into their living room every night after the children went to bed. Christians routinely subscribe to cable and Internet services that bring graphic immorality one click of a remote control or mouse button away.

Three high school students, all Christians and from Christian families, spent the evening in one of their homes watching two video movies. Parents also watched snatches of them. Both movies were rated R and contained sexually explicit language and crude sex scenes. The parents shook their heads in disgust a few times but didn't want to "spoil the fun," so said nothing.

I've been in several Christian homes where one look in the bedrooms of the teenage sons reveals the best selling sex symbol posters on the market, rivaling the pornographic foldouts of a generation ago. Computers and Internet connections behind closed bedroom doors are nearly as common in Christian homes as in non-Christian. My novel *Lord Foulgrin's Letters* demonstrates the impact this has on one family.

Like the frog that boiled to death by degrees, many Christian homes have been gradually desensitized to sexual sin. The result is predictable—immorality is more rampant among believers than ever before.

Immorality in the Holy Church of God

A 23-year-old boy announces to his parents, "I'm gay." A man comes home from a business trip to find his 17-year-old daughter in bed with a boy she's been dating three weeks. A woman comes home from shopping to find her six-year-old daughter and a teenage neighbor boy naked and fondling each other. A father of two has sex with the 16-year-old babysitter. A highschooler admits to his unsuspecting parents that he is a prostitute. These things didn't just happen; they happened in Christian families. I know, because they came to me for help.

When we hear that 70 percent of young people engage in sexual intercourse before marriage, most of us assume our own church young people constitute the other 30 percent. But any youth pastor in touch with reality will tell you this is often not the case.

Jim was a high school sophomore, from a Christian family, active in his youth group. His first sexual experience was at a Christian summer camp. Linda also had premarital sex at a Christian camp—with one of the counselors.

Dave became a Christian as a 22-year-old. He made such great spiritual strides that he assumed he would never fall back to his former lifestyle. Yet one day he found himself committing adultery with a woman he'd been witnessing to.

Susan was also a strong Christian. One evening, seemingly without warning, she fell back into sexual sin. Later, in a small group Bible study, she volunteered to the rest of us, "I didn't know I needed to be on guard against immorality. I thought being a Christian made it impossible to go back to that again. When I fell, I was shocked and devastated. I really didn't believe it could happen to me. But it did."

Endowed with exceptional intelligence, attractiveness, and athletic skill, Brian was a leader in the youth group. He charmed the whole church with his exciting testimony. But time brought a gradual erosion of Brian's moral standards. It surfaced in his words, his clothing, his body language, and his choice of friends. Now in his twenties, Brian recently boasted to a friend, "I can get any girl I want in bed with me."

Cindy is a Christian girl whose fiancé broke up with her and dropped out of church, disillusioned with the Christian life. When I asked her why, her matter-of-fact reply took me by surprise—"I think it began when I seduced him." She went on to say, "At first he didn't want to have sex, but I talked him into it. After that, sex was all he could think about. Then he got bitter at me and at God, and now he's really messed up."

Adultery in the Church

Linda, a mother of four in her middle thirties, had just discovered she was pregnant again. But there was a complication. The child's father was the man who lived next door, not her husband. "Should I get an abortion?" she asked with alarming ease and sincerity.

Debbie's situation was similar to Linda's—she was uncertain whether her baby's father was her husband or one of their friends at church with whom she said she had "slipped up."

John and Pat came into my office with the vague diagnosis of "marriage problems." When I met with each separately, John described himself as "a man of strong biblical convictions which is the only thing keeping me from divorcing Pat." Later John admitted he had been unfaithful to Pat and had carried on "a few affairs" behind her back. "How many affairs?" I asked. "Six," he replied, with a slight blush (they had been married only eight years).

I was asked to confront a man who was resisting a Christian woman's attempt to break off their adulterous affair. I called the man and was surprised when he assured me, despite his adultery, "I want you to know that I'm a Christian, and I regularly pray that Joel [the woman's husband] will come to Christ."

Other Sexual Perversions in the Church

Nicolle, a young Christian wife, tearfully confessed that her husband had hounded her to go to bed with him and another woman. At first she refused, but in tired frustration she finally gave in. To say the least, she was sorry.

Melinda called late one night and began, "I'm ashamed to even ask this. But what should I do if I think my husband is fooling around with our three-year-old daughter?" Her husband was a professing believer—an alumnus of a fine Christian college.

Fran was raped as a six-year-old by her grandfather, and again when she was eleven by the father of children she was babysitting. Both men were faithful churchgoers.

Tom and Betty, parents of four, were active lay leaders in their church. They came to me—on the verge of divorce—because Tom was sexually involved with his sister.

A friend told me that his church just went through a scandal that rocked the community. A 14 year-old girl was pregnant by her grandfather—one of the church's elders.

Immorality in the Ministry

"Randy, something terrible has happened here at the church," said my friend, calling from another state. "Yesterday, one of the pastors left his wife and ran off with another woman." I was sorry; but not shocked or even surprised. Thirty years ago I would have been shocked; fifteen years ago I would have been surprised. Now I was sad. I have heard the same story too many times to be surprised ever again.

A veteran seminary professor was dismissed for immorality. After accepting a pastorate in another part of the country, his ordination was revoked because of further sexual sin.

When I spoke for a week at a Bible college, many students came for counseling. Among them were Pam, Barb, and Rachel. Pam said she went to her church's staff counselor for help in dealing with insecurities tied to childhood abuse by her father. This counselor was the first man Pam had ever been able to trust. Two months later he convinced her to have sex with him. Eighteen-year-old Barb is the daughter of a deacon at an evangelical church who for years sexually abused Barb and her two younger sisters. Rachel confessed through a flood of tears that she came to Bible school to escape an ongoing affair with the senior pastor of her church.

Eighteen-year-old Toni, also a Bible college student, told me she committed immorality with her former youth pastor. The church never found this out, but it was not long before the pastor involved moved on to a new ministry. Toni's primary concern, however, did not relate to this former youth pastor but to her current affair with the church's new youth pastor (both men were married and had young children). Toni gave me permission to discuss her problem with the school's dean of women.

"What is going on with Christian leaders anymore?" asked this woman counselor. "Last year our music minister was dismissed for adultery—not only at our church but at several previous ones. But what really hurts," she went on, "is what happened to the head of the Bible department at my alma mater, a man I have known and respected for years. Six months ago the school had to fire him because he committed adultery. Since then, he divorced his wife and married the other woman!"

Most of these tragedies are kept as quiet as possible to save churches, Christian organizations, and individuals from embarrassment. Many others have made their way to the public eye, however. In past years these have included a leading Bible college president running off with a student, a pastor engaged in homosexual activities with young boys at his church, and an evangelist found murdered in the bed of his partner in adultery. And, of course, there were the well-known televangelist scandals of the late 1980s.

One of the most widely publicized cases was that of a nationally known crusader for Christian morality and president of a prominent Christian college. *Time* magazine revealed this man had been sexually involved with at least five students at his college, four of them men, over a period of three years. This Christian leader, who blamed his behavior on "genes and chromosomes," publicly denounced sexual immorality right up to the day he was exposed.

Leadership magazine printed a lengthy article entitled, "The War Within: An Anatomy of Lust." The author's name was withheld. We know only that he is a Christian leader who describes in detail his ten year slavery to lust, from which he was recently delivered. This is how he begins:

> I am writing this article anonymously because I am embarrassed. Embarrassed for my wife and children, yes, but embarrassed most for myself. I will tell of my personal battle with lust, and if I believed I was the only one who fought in that war, I would not waste emotional energy dredging up stained and painful memories. But I believe my experience is not uncommon, is perhaps even typical of pastors, writers, and conference speakers. No one talks about it. No one writes about it. But it's there, like an unacknowledged cancer that metastasizes best when no one goes for x-rays or feels for lumps.[7]

Though I would not call his experience typical, it is undoubtedly more common than any of us would like to believe. Scandals involving television evangelists and well known pastors have plagued us for the past fifteen years.

Certainly, I have no wish to cast suspicion on Christian leaders or malign the reputation of the ministry I am part of. Many men and women in Christian ministry are shining examples of personal holiness. But a significant and growing number *are* succumbing to sexual immorality—-tragically illustrating the need to devote unprecedented thought and effort to this issue.

Where Does This Leave Us?

One day when I was a pastor, two of my three afternoon appointments began with confessions of adultery. The third involved the most deeply rooted and sordid history of homosexual behavior I have ever encountered. All three counselees were professing Christians—and in only one of them did I sense genuine repentance, though sin had wreaked havoc in each of their lives.

Fifteen years ago in a six-day span, I faced the following counseling appointments: a 40 year old man who slept with a woman he met at a home Bible study; a middle-aged woman who left her husband to live with another man for two years; a young married man emotionally wrapped up with his secretary and contemplating divorcing his wife for her; a college student who had participated in a homosexual act with a man instrumental in his conversion; a Christian woman pursuing an affair with her church's deacon board chairman. Of the ten people involved in sin, only two were non-Christians.

In the subsequent years I have asked myself a sobering question: For every Christian family I know of that has been devastated by immorality, how many tens of thousands more are there? I can only conclude that for decades we have been facing among Christians a moral epidemic of enormous and frightening proportions.

Despite the life-changing power that is fully available to us in Christ, despite the fact that many Christian families are experiencing unprecedented spiritual and moral victory, the problems that we face have never been greater.

Enslaved by sexual sin in mind and body, plagued and haunted by its guilt, innumerable children of God are tragically incapacitated in their attempts to live for Christ. Nothing so hamstrings the believer's spiritual potency as sexual compromise—and never has the Church in America been so compromised as now.

I know there is risk in putting such things in print. Yet I believe there is much more to be lost by keeping silent. We can no longer afford the luxury of naiveté in this critical area. Furthermore, it is impossible to overestimate the damage done to the cause of Christ by the sexual impurity of his people. The Church's impact on a dark world is lost when believers attempt to straddle a spiritual no man's land, with one foot on the narrow path of Christ and the other on the broad highway of the world. The more muddled the line between world and Church, the more bleak the future of both.

Just as certainly, however, this moral tragedy can be turned into spiritual triumph. The Church's sexual purity could once again become her trademark—a reminder that Church and world are not the same and that those weary of the world may find not only peace, but purity in the Church.

The Good News: There's Hope!

In the fifteen years since I wrote the first edition of this book, some things have gotten much worse. (For example, the threat to purity posed by the accessibility of pornography over the Internet.) But other things have gotten better. In many churches and Christian families, the tide is showing some signs of turning.

When I first wrote, very few churches addressed the subject of lust and sexual purity from the pulpit. Now this is being done much more often, though it is still off limits in some churches (which, predictably, results in the problem being more widespread). While very little had been written on purity before, many good books and articles have been written since.

When this book was published, my church had, since its beginning in 1977, women's retreats every year, but never had a men's retreat or special meetings for men of any kind. In 1988 we had our first men's retreat. I spoke on sexual purity. I asked eight men, whose stories I knew, to give their testimonies at various points, telling how they had struggled with pornography and sexual temptation, and how God was giving them victory. We all left that retreat blown away by the stories, with renewed hope and encouragement. Many men said, "I thought I was the only one who struggled. I'd given up hope that anyone could understand, or that I could do anything to find victory."

Since the men's movement of the early '90s, my church and many others now have men's meetings and small groups where men ask each other pointed questions and truly hold each other accountable in many area, including sexual purity.

Depending on which surveys you believe, the rate of casual teen sex—while still alarmingly high—has apparently decreased some. There has definitely been a resurgence of popularity in virginity. In 1985 "virgin" was a name some teens called others, now many young people are proud of their virginity and openly talk of saving themselves until marriage. Even several professional athletes have been outspoken advocates of abstinence until marriage.

My daughters were little girls fifteen years ago. By the time they got to junior high and high school, our church youth groups were putting a major emphasis on sexual purity. They had their own retreats, one for girls only, one for guys only, where youth workers and parents openly told their stories and directly addressed the importance of sexual purity and how to maintain it.

Before either of my girls ever dated a boy, I developed a twelve-page handout of guidelines for sexual purity. Before any boy could date one of my girls, he and I and my wife and daughter had to meet together and go through this handout point by point, Scripture by Scripture. We openly discussed our expectations, and the standards we expected to be maintained. Many parents, hearing about this process, asked for these guidelines, and many have used them with their own children. I've since heard of others across the country doing the same things, with their own sets of standards. Fifteen years ago this was very rare.

Instead of peer pressure toward moral compromise, our church youth groups provide a peer pressure toward sexual purity. When someone suggests going to a certain movie, it's not unusual for others to speak up for purity and influence the group toward a different choice. While many Christian youth are still tragically succumbing to the world's pressure to surrender their virginity, many youth pastors will tell you there's now a sharper distinction than ever between the rate of purity among committed church kids and the world.

Sex Respect and other abstinence programs have made their way not only into churches and Christian schools, but many public schools. The concept of "secondary virginity," committing yourself to never again surrender your purity, has gained widespread acceptance. I have stood in front of a large crowd of highschoolers, speaking on sexual purity, then inviting them to come forward and put on a necklace or ring to demonstrate their commitment to purity. I've seen 90% of the young people come forward. This wasn't happening fifteen years ago. The extreme popularity among youth of Josh Harris's book *I Kissed Dating Goodbye* is another evidence of a fresh openness among young people to pursue lifestyle alternatives that preserve and protect their purity.

I receive many letters from young people regarding my book *ProLife Answers to ProChoice Arguments* and my novels such as *Deadline*, which deal with moral issues. Many of these youth state that they are committed to sexual purity. I've seen school newspaper editorials advocating abstinence. Christian young people give speeches on this topic. They speak up in public school classrooms, taking issue with teachers who advocate moral relativists, and speakers from Planned Parenthood who try to spoon-feed them the hand-kids-a-condom philosophy that's the equivalent of saying, "We'll teach you how to dodge cars on the freeway." The young people are saying, "No thanks—we're choosing to stay off the freeway in the first place."

More parents are turning away from passivity and its devastating consequences. They're taking charge of their families, monitoring or removing the televisions and Internet connections. They're protecting their children from immoral relationships, guarding them from impure influences, and talking with them ultimately to cultivate their own moral convictions.

A few minutes ago, while I was writing this section, I took a break, walking from my office to my house. My wife said, "I've just had two phone calls I have to tell you about." Both calls reinforced the major themes of this chapter.

The first concerned a man in our church who's very respected and has taught classes and led Bible studies. He's one of the last people you'd expect to leave his wife, but that's what he's done. The good news was, two men went to him, men who've been involved with him in an accountability group. Another man also confronted him, challenging him to turn from his sin and repent. His own son, coming from a youth group that upholds purity and obedience, confronted him with the truth. I don't know how this will turn out. I'm troubled by the man's sin, of course, but such things are nothing new. What is new and refreshing is the biblical conviction and spiritual power with which other men, including his son, went to confront him and hold him to a clear biblical standard.

The other phone call was from a Christian woman who'd been living in immorality for some time. She called to say she was moving out of her boyfriend's house and breaking off their relationship. Why? Because other Christian women had talked to her, and she was finally convicted that this was wrong and God has something better for her. The move made her life complicated for several reasons, including financial ones, but she decided the cost of impurity was too high, and she wanted God's best for her life. Encouraged by others who loved her enough to tell her the truth, she was rejecting the world's way and embracing God's.

So, while every day many people are turning from sexual purity, many others are simultaneously turning toward it. My hope is that this book will help turn the tide further, so that moral tragedy can be turned into spiritual triumph. My prayer is that the Church's sexual purity could once again become her trademark.

May we be reminded that Church and world are not the same. May we see with clarity that the Church must make a conscious prayerful effort to resist the world's influence, drawing on all the strength of the risen Christ.

May those weary of the world, tired of the oppressive burden of immorality, find in the Church not only the peace but the purity they long for.

It is God's will that you should be sanctified: that you should avoid sexual immorality; that each of you should learn to control his own body in a way that is holy and honorable, not in passionate lust like the heathen, who do not know God; and that in this matter no one should wrong his brother or take advantage of him. The Lord will punish men for all such sins, as we have already told you and warned you. For God did not call us to be impure, but to live a holy life. Therefore, he who rejects this instruction does not reject man but God, who gives you his Holy Spirit. (1 Thessalonians 4:3-8)

Chapter 1, Notes

1. John Leo, "In Search of Sexual Desire" *Time*, 4 April 1983, 80.
2. Carin Rubenstein, "The Modem Art of Courtly Love," *Psychology Today*, July 1983, 40.
3. Peter Marin, "A Revolution's Broken Promises," *Psychology Today*, July 1983,51-57.
4. A. W Tozer, *Born After Midnight* (Harrisburg, Penn.: Christian Publications, Inc., 1959), 36.
5. Ibid., 37.
6. John White, *Flirting with the World* (Wheaton, IL.: Harold Shaw Publishers, 1982),75, 81.
7. *The Oregonian*, 14 July 1984.
8. "The War Within: An Anatomy of Lust," *Leadership*, Fall 1982, 31.

CHAPTER 2

The Whos, Hows, and Whys of the Sexual Revolution

In 1956, Harvard sociologist Pitirim Sorokin stated:

This sex revolution is as important as the most dramatic political or economic upheaval. It is changing the lives of men and women more radically than any other revolution of our time. . . .

Any considerable change in marriage behavior, any increase in sexual promiscuity and illicit relations, is pregnant with momentous consequences. A sex revolution drastically affects the lives of millions, deeply disturbs the community, and decisively influences the future of society.[1]

Any movement this significant deserves our attention. In order to respond to the new world created by the sexual revolution, it is important to know its history—how and why it happened. These wholesale changes in our nation's sexual morality did not appear overnight. They are the cumulative product of significant people, ideas, forces, and events. If we understand them better, it may help us make our own impact for good on the course of moral history.

UNDERSTANDING THE REVOLUTION

Every revolution is against some established order. The American sexual revolution's assault was on the nation's order of sexual mores. These mores were firmly rooted in the Judeo-Christian ethic, itself founded on the teachings of the Bible.

As we will see in later chapters, the Bible affirms personal chastity, modesty, fidelity, and marriage as the only proper context for sexual intimacy. It unapologetically condemns pre-marital sex (fornication), extramarital sex (adultery), homo-sexual relations, incest, and all other sexual behavior outside of marriage. Furthermore, it condemns sexual lust (not desires, but mental indulgences) and sees it as the root of all immoral behavior.

Before the sexual revolution, most Americans affirmed this biblical sexual ethic, with all its social and legal implications. Some of the same, of course, violated this ethic in private. But it is important to understand that the sexual revolution did not simply produce more infringements on the established moral standard. Rather, it changed the standard itself. Hence, as do all true revolutions, this one altered not only actions but attitudes, not simply behavior but belief. The sexual revolution was fundamentally a revolution not of the body, but of the mind.

Sexual Negativism in the Church

Throughout much of Church history a dark cloud hovered over sex. Church fathers like Chrysostom and Jerome spoke demeaningly of sex, even in marriage. Origen taught that sex was inherently wrong; Augustine, that sex was part of the original sin of Genesis 3—despite the command to procreate in Genesis 1 and the one flesh marital relationship of Genesis 2.[2]

Such unbiblical perspectives led to equating celibacy with spirituality and advocating sexless marriage, in direct contradiction of the New Testament (1 Corinthians 7:3-5).

As a whole, Luther and the other reformers were milder in their disregard for sex, but negative nonetheless. Later the Puritans gained a reputation for sexual austerity, epitomized in the man who allegedly had his wife executed for smiling during intercourse.

Actually, the Puritans are victims of bad press—as a whole they made real strides toward a healthy view of sex within marriage. On one occasion, for instance, a man was disciplined by a Puritan church for refusing to have sex with his wife.[3] Many Puritans held to a positive view of sex in marriage, and, like the biblical writers, considered that view totally consistent with condemning sex outside marriage.

In contrast, the Victorian age was notoriously hypocritical. Sexual purity was outwardly elevated, yet married men were permitted to consort with prostitutes, partly to save their wives from the "indignity" of sex (how noble of them). As has often been the case in human history, where sex was demeaned, sexual immorality was prevalent.

In her zeal to hold the line against immorality, the Church miserably failed to embrace or project a positive view of sex. This failure contributed to the sexual pressure cooker that finally exploded in the form of the sexual revolution.

The Church's antisexual posture was ultimately antihuman, since people are sexual beings. That posture not only set the stage for the sexual revolution but caused the Church to be caught flat-footed when the revolution came. By the time the Church's head cleared and it said, "Really, it's not sex we're against, but the misuse of sex," no one was listening. Had the Church all along taught a positive view of sex (see chapter 7), she could have taken the wind out of the sexual revolution's sails—and saved herself, and perhaps a good deal of society, from the great sex swindle of recent years.

The Birth of Secularism

The Renaissance, the transitional period between the Middle Ages and the modern era, was a time of great creativity and accomplishment in the arts and sciences. It marked the birth of humanism, of emphasis on human potential.

Later came the Enlightenment, an eighteenth century philosophic movement marked by individualism, scientific empiricism, the questioning of traditional doctrines and values, and the exaltation of human reason. Through the Enlightenment, humanism degenerated into secularism. God's moral laws (not least those pertaining to sex) were questioned, reinterpreted, and, increasingly, considered less relevant to modern man, who saw himself as coming of age and capable of making his own moral decisions.

Charles Darwin's *Origin of Species* (1859) was an historic landmark, not simply in biology but in philosophy and theology. The theory of evolution fit secularism like a glove. Man was already asserting his intellectual and moral independence from God. Evolution provided the missing link—a sense of physical independence from God. After all, if God was not man's physical Creator, how could he be his moral judge? Man was seen as the determiner of his own destiny, the architect of his own moral standards. No longer in need of a Creator, he was no longer in need of standards foisted upon him by a Creator.

While at first the masses resisted the nontheistic implications of evolution, the intellectual elite welcomed it. It was for them, pardon the expression, an answer to prayer.

INFLUENTIAL PEOPLE

Sigmund Freud

Sigmund Freud was to psychology what Darwin was to biology. Freud researched and counseled in Vienna at the end of the nineteenth century in the sexually neurotic and hypocritical climate of Victorianism. There he witnessed sexual repression in the extreme.

It was on this loom of sexual repression that Freud wove his revolutionary ideas of human sexuality. Had he found instead a Church that fostered in society a healthy view of sex in marriage, his findings would have been much different—and we probably wouldn't know his name.

Freud came to see sex as basic to all human needs, drives

and problems. He popularized new concepts and terms like "libido," "id," "ego," "super-ego," and "psychic energy." He fathered the famous Oedipal concept, which effectively placed the blame for incest on the child's desire to seduce the parent of the opposite sex. Freud was the first to legitimize sex both as a field of research and a topic of conversation.

Freud's pioneer research was influenced by his own sexual quirks. These included not only impotence, but incestuous and homosexual tendencies.[4] None of this minimizes Freud's unquestionable brilliance and immense contributions to human understanding. It simply points out—as does our knowledge of other sexual reformers—that it is difficult to separate one's sexual beliefs from his sexual experiences.

Freud's views often conflicted with Christian theology. He believed neither in God nor the after-life, and acknowledged his debt to Darwin in molding some of his most basic convictions. Freud's ideas tremendously influenced the directions of psychology, counseling, education, and even religion. It would be difficult to overestimate his role in the development of twentieth century Western thought.

Havelock Ellis

Havelock Ellis, also highly influenced by Darwin and once a disciple of Freud, carried considerable clout in the early stages of the sexual revolution. The seven volumes of his *Studies in the Psychology of Sex*, published between 1897 and 1928, were banned in England, and available in the United States only to the medical profession until 1935.

Why the furor over Ellis's writings? He was one of the first influential figures to publicly recommend premarital sex.

Before the 1920s he defended the legitimacy of nonlegal unions, the same arrangements dubbed "living together" in the sixties. He also strongly opposed the existing legislation that made sexual relations with a girl under twenty-one illegal, arguing that if such an age was necessary, which he doubted, it should not exceed sixteen.

Havelock Ellis was the international hero of the contraceptive crusade. He was also a firm believer in eugenics, advocating voluntary sterilization of the genetically "inferior," and mandatory sterilization of the "feeble-minded." His position was logically rooted in the Darwinian concept of man, especially the concepts of natural selection and the survival of the fittest. He was committed to the secularist doctrine of man's ability and, indeed, destiny to control himself and his environment in producing the highest form of humanity.

Ellis's research in homosexuality was done with John Addington Symonds, himself a homosexual. Most of the case studies were from the experiences of Symonds and his homosexual partners.[5] Others came from Havelock's own wife Edith's lesbian relationships, which he not only knew about, but encouraged.[6] Not surprisingly, Ellis became convinced that homosexuality was neither a disease nor a crime, a position assumed by many today, but almost unheard of before Ellis. Indeed, his famous work *Sexual Inversion* was more a piece of propaganda than serious research:

> Although cast in the form of a scientific treatise, the book was in essence an apology for homosexuality—a classic example of Ellis's lifelong effort to broaden the spectrum of acceptable sexual behavior . . . all served to create an impression of homosexuality as an innocuous departure

from the sexual norm, and one not without its advantages for society.[7]

Bertrand Russell

Perhaps no scholar ever wrote so prolifically in such diverse fields as Nobel prizewinner Bertrand Russell. Able to tackle the realms of philosophy, science, mathematics, history, education, politics, religion, and ethics, he is widely regarded as the greatest intellectual of the twentieth century. Not the least of his lasting efforts was invested in purging us of our Judeo-Christian morality.

Russell was more active than Ellis in advocating trial marriage. He promoted "companionate marriage" in his *Marriage and Morals* (1929), maintaining that entering into marriage without sexual involvement was "just as absurd as it would be if a man intending to buy a house were not allowed to view it until he had completed the purchase." He also proposed, "No marriage should be legally binding until the wife's first pregnancy."[8]

Russell's personal life was as unconventional as his writings. In 1910, he left his wife for another woman. The years ahead brought three divorces and three more marriages, as well as several other affairs.

Margaret Sanger

In her own way, Margaret Sanger eclipsed both Ellis and Russell in her influence on the sexual mores of America. Though not the first advocate of family limitation, her untiring efforts justly earned her the title "the mother of birth control." She established the first birth control clinic in 1916 in Brooklyn, founded the American Birth Control League, organized the first World Population Conference in Geneva in 1922, and was the first president of the International Planned Parenthood Federation, founded in 1953. She served as Planned Parenthood's honorary chairman until her death in 1966. Wherever Planned Parenthood exercises its worldwide influence today, it bears the undying signature of Margaret Sanger.

Sanger tied the issue of contraceptives to the issue of women's rights. She was the predecessor of today's millions of Americans who see abortion as a woman's personal right, rooted in her equality and freedom of choice.

Sanger's *Pivot of Civilization* is a blueprint for changing the world through birth control and sterilization, both voluntary and involuntary. The book is a clear and direct application of Darwinian nontheistic evolutionary dogma.[9] Often portrayed today—particularly by Planned Parenthood—as the compassionate champion of the underprivileged, Sanger was really an elitist who labeled the masses "genetically inferior" and "human weeds."[10] "Funds that should be used to raise the standard of our civilization are diverted to the maintenance of those who should never have been born," Sanger complained. "More children from the fit, less from the unfit—that is the chief issue of birth control."[11] Like Ellis, Sanger saw eugenics—the genetic improvement and purification of the human race—as the ultimate purpose of birth control.

Sanger's personal life was consistent with her philosophy. Married three times (including an early "trial marriage"), she was involved in frequent adulterous relationships. Among her better-known lovers were H. G. Wells and. . . Havelock Ellis.

The Ellis-Russell-Sanger Connection

Havelock Ellis, Bertrand Russell, and Margaret Sanger shared in common a bitter disdain for the sexual values of the Christian faith. All three were prominent in what was then called the League for Sexual Reform. All three drew upon their gifts, skills, resources, and fame to promote a new sexual philosophy and lifestyle. Americans were gradually desensitized to their ideas which, in time, no longer seemed so radical and offensive. Eventually, they became agreeable, appealing, and widely accepted.

Ellis, Russell, and Sanger opened the floodgates for the speeches and writings of a whole new breed of intellectual and social reformers. By the 1930s these revolutionaries were defending not only premarital sex, living together, and temporal marriage contracts, but the legitimacy of prostitution, homosexuality, adultery, and abortion on demand.

It must be emphasized again that this sexual revolution was directly and knowingly aimed against the authority of God, the Bible, and the Church. In reading Ellis, Russell, and Sanger, I am struck with their frequent, hostile, and bitter castigations of Christian faith and morality. Margaret Sanger said it clearly on the masthead of *The Woman Rebel:* "No gods, no masters."

Denouncing "all ethical systems which rest upon unquestioning obedience of higher authorities," she stated:

> There has been a revolution in the world of morality of which we are now beginning to taste the first fruits. We are no longer living in a little closed and completed universe of which God's plan was revealed once and for all time to a lit-

tle group of delegates. The center of our universe has shifted from Heaven to earth.[12]

Where the dogmatists read black, the world today is reading white. What they consider "morality" we consider moral imbecility.[13]

In her 1938 autobiography, Sanger penned words that could well have been the slogan of the sexual revolution that followed her: "Let God and man decree laws for themselves and not for me."[14]

THE UNDERMINING OF BIBLICAL MORALITY

As secularism spread, the biblical foundations for sexual morality were undermined. "Because the Bible says so" was no longer a good enough answer to the question, "Why shouldn't I have sex outside marriage?"

In the early twentieth century, most people outwardly conformed to the Judeo-Christian ethic. In reality, however, sexual morality was chiefly grounded not on the fear of God but on three other fears: (1) Fear of detection (discovery normally meant rejection and punishment); (2) fear of infection (venereal disease); and (3) fear of conception (unwanted pregnancy). As these moral policemen declined in power, so did the observance of biblical morality.

The 1920s saw increasing freedom, affluence, and, with the advent of cars, mobility. All this made the detection of immorality more preventable. Meanwhile, the gradual erosion of values made detection less traumatic even when it did occur.

Medical science was making great strides in combating venereal disease with antibiotics. Though V.D. was still a major health problem, the fear of infection was waning.

The greatest fear and deterrent to immorality, unwanted pregnancy, was addressed by birth control. The late nineteenth century brought the first reliable contraceptives, but it was not until the 1920s that they became increasingly available to the general public. Nonabortive birth control may have had a positive and legitimate use, a subject hotly debated in the Christian community. However, its most noticeable effect was vesting extramarital sex with unprecedented impunity. It was more than a notion of male supremacy that bred the famous double standard in which nice women were expected to be chaste while "nice" men consorted with immoral women. All along, the fear of pregnancy gave women a special incentive (unshared by men) to avoid premarital sex. Birth control changed all the rules.

Much of the women's rights movement was long overdue. Unfortunately, promiscuity became a proving ground for women's rights. The double standard was rightly deplored. But instead of attacking the double standard by crusading for male chastity, the women's movement encouraged female extramarital sex. The liberating result was that more women acted immorally (resulting, of course, in more available partners and therefore still higher immorality in men). Morally speaking, it was as if women achieved equality with men by jumping off a ten story building to join them on the pavement below.

The Moral Erosion of the Twenties

That birth control could usher in a new morality shows how weak the average citizen's moral foundation had already become. But we must remember that much of society was accepting Darwinian thought, including its implicit lack of accountability to any authority. Scholars in every field were working overtime attempting to disprove the Bible. Psychologists were relieving patients of their sexual repressions and inhibitions. Social activists were pushing for a new age, characterized by a new creed and a new lifestyle. Founded in 1920, the American Civil Liberties Union was already stripping legal standards of their Christian implications. As society's controlling force, Judeo-Christian morality already had one foot in the grave. Birth control simply hastened its funeral.

The waters of biology, philosophy, psychology, education, medicine, and other disciplines converged into a unified torrent that pummeled the nation's moral dam. The result was the first great phase of the American sexual revolution—the "roaring twenties":

> In the 1920s, a radical change occurred almost overnight. The belief became a militant dogma in liberal circles that the opposite of repression—namely sex education, freedom of talking, feeling and expression—would have healthy effects and obviously constituted the only stand for the enlightened person. In an amazingly short period following World War I, we shifted from acting as though sex did not exist at all to being obsessed with it.[15]

With the war over, there was a sense of relief, relaxation, and celebration. The jazz age was born, bootleg liquor was plentiful, parties flourished, inhibitions dropped.

The economic struggle of the Great Depression, followed by the buildup to World War II, temporarily quieted the rebellious spirit of the roaring twenties. But not before they provided a preview of the coming sixties.

The Kinsey Reports

In 1948 Alfred Kinsey startled the country with his *Sexual Behavior and the Human Male*. He followed with *Sexual Behavior and the Human Female* in 1953. The reports were based on 10,000 personal interviews with American men and women—and went about as unnoticed as Pearl Harbor.

For the first time, people were able to look into the bedrooms of the rest of the nation. What they had always wondered about the sex lives of others, they were now told. And what they found was that sexual standards were far more liberal than they thought.

When sex was put in a goldfish bowl for all to gawk at, several significant things happened. People began to compare themselves with each other. Many concluded they were undersexed. After all, Kinsey said three quarters of the males questioned had premarital sex, half of those married had committed adultery, and a third had at least one homosexual experience since puberty. Half the women had experienced premarital intercourse, and a quarter of those married had committed adultery. The sheer weight of the numbers lessened immorality's stigma. "Everybody's doing it, or at least many people are, so why not me?"

Kinsey's data were widely disseminated in the press, and for the first time, people in the United States were confronted with the wide gap between their sexual practices and their sexual mores. One probable effect of these studies was that many people became more free in their sexual behavior—or at least felt less guilty about it—secure in the knowledge that they were joining sizeable numbers of other citizens.[16]

Ironically, Kinsey's figures almost certainly exaggerated the moral looseness of the day. Most of those interviewed were college students, the most liberal section of the populace at probably the most liberal period in their lives. It also seems likely that those who volunteered for detailed interviews about their sex lives were the most sexually experienced. Whether accurate or not, the Kinsey reports were believed. Sexual experiences became fair game even for casual conversation. A lunch table discussion could now begin, "So what do you think of the Kinsey reports?"

Kinsey also opened the door for later researchers like William Masters and Virginia Johnson, who in the sixties and early seventies wrote *Human Sexual Response, Human Sexual Inadequacy,* and *The Pleasure Bond.* Masters and Johnson didn't just update Kinsey's poll—they observed and studied men and women in actual sexual experiences, using sophisticated electronic equipment to measure sexual stimulation and reactions. They even used an artificial "coition machine," simulating intercourse.

Between Kinsey's reports and the research of Masters and Johnson, people increasingly looked at sex as a thing, an entity that could be scrutinized, weighed, and measured. Sex was now in the hands of science, not ethics. Sex was classified, objectified, and depersonalized. Like a bacteria culture, it was put under the microscope and then on the display table.

More and more sex manuals were written stressing sex

habits, idiosyncrasies, techniques, and positions—and ignoring the personal, moral, and spiritual dimensions of sex. If there were any mystery left in sex, which was increasingly doubtful, it seemed destined to soon be discovered, probably in a test tube. Then, no doubt, it would be patented, bottled, and distributed in supermarkets. In short, sex was stripped of its magic. It was no longer sacred.

Winds of Change in the 1950s

Moving back to the Kinsey era, it was 1952 that brought the first widely publicized sex change operation. Christina Jorgensen became a household name. Some shuddered, some applauded, some laughed—all who paused to think saw that medical science was bringing unprecedented implications to traditional morality.

The fifties also brought the influential voice of Margaret Mead. An anthropologist who studied preliterate societies like those in New Guinea, Mead lectured and wrote about the cultural conditioning of sexual behavior. America's traditional sexual mores were by no means universal. The noble savage had fewer taboos and seemed happier than we. Minds were open to new value systems, gleaned from the remote corners of the global village. In recent years, many of Mead's findings have been called into serious question. Nonetheless, they significantly impacted our thinking.

The fifties brought an increasing sense of nonaccountability to anyone but self. The "'sacrifice for others" spirit of World War II gave way in the post-war prosperity to selfishness and personal ambition. Many of the children raised in this climate (influenced by the liberal theories of Dr. Benjamin Spock, which he later recanted) would grow up to be takers, not givers, largely indifferent to their responsibilities and preoccupied with their rights.

The fifties beat movement preached alienation from the older generation, derisively called "squares." The "hip" beatniks glorified personal freedom, enlightenment, and expression through heightened sensory awareness. This was induced by a blend of jazz music, poetry, sex, drugs, and gleanings from Zen Buddhism. The beat movement was ingrown, egocentric, and limited in influence. Still, its anti-establishment mentality, experimentation with drugs and sex, and its own distinctive music were a foretaste of the sixties.

American youth were gaining freedom. More high school and college students had access to cars. Parking and necking were popular sports, performed to the background music of Fabian, Ricky Nelson, Buddy Holly, and Elvis Presley (the most potent youth sex symbol ever).

Drugs, Sex, and Rock 'N' Roll

By the sixties the generation gap was established, the seeds of rebellion sown. The youth revolution lacked only leaders, visible and charismatic leaders who could symbolize the odyssey of youth in search of a new moral philosophy and lifestyle.

In 1964 those leaders emerged—the Beatles. Their records sold millions overnight. The radios of a whole generation were tuned to their songs. Girls screamed and fainted at their concerts, while parents shook their heads and wondered. Few suspected that this unlikely band from Liverpool would prove to be among the most effective propagandists of this century.

Within a few years the Beatles were the high priests of a

youth kingdom built on drugs, sex, and rock. Their biographies and personal interviews attest to the free sex and frequent orgies that characterized their tours. Three of them married girlfriends already pregnant. They sang, "Why don't we do it in the road"—not about skateboarding. Later, leader John Lennon and future wife Yoko Ono appeared nude, front and back, on the album "Two Virgins." Not an apt title, since at the time the two were known bedpartners, and John was still married to another woman.

The Beatles were accompanied by groups like the Rolling Stones, dominated by lead singer Mick Jagger. His sensuous presence and sexually explicit actions on stage electrified the crowds. He sang, "I Can't Get No Satisfaction," and followed with a string of other hits that flouted sexual taboos, including "Let's Spend the Night Together."

While an already waning Christian morality went into eclipse, America's youth worshiped at the shrine of a new god, an indivisible trinity of drugs, sex, and rock. The winds of change that had blown since the twenties became a hurricane on the shoulders of the sixties' youth culture.

The sexual revolution was but one facet of a total revolution against established authority. Though the hippies spoke earnestly of love, sex was as much an act of rebellion as love— "See, we'll do what we want, and you can't stop us." In 1969 the famous rock festival Woodstock showed the other side of the free sex movement. Billed as a foretaste of utopia, for many it degenerated into a miserable orgy of filth, disease, drugs, and sexual perversion.

Ironically, though the hippie movement would pass, within a decade, its radical sexual morality would infiltrate the mainstream of American society.

America's New Moral Climate

The sixties were days of change. The birth rate plunged, and the divorce rate soared. Nudist colonies popped up like lemonade stands in summer. Overage hippie Timothy Leary told *Playboy* that LSD was the key to female orgasm (a claim that failed to win him the Nobel prize). Most remarkable was the popularization of "sexual freedom" by society's influential elite—the intellectuals, professors, philosophers, psychologists, and writers.

By 1970 professors at Long Beach State were showing their classes actual films of heterosexual and homosexual intercourse. Planned Parenthood was invited to high schools all over the nation, showing 16-year-old sophomores how to obtain and use birth control devices. After the Supreme Court legalized abortion in 1973, school counselors acted as liaisons between teenage girls and abortion clinics.

None of this could have happened without one dominant force: the American media. As bees spread pollen, the nation's newspapers, magazines, books, movies, and television spread the changing values. They were the winged messengers and mouthpieces of the sexual revolution.

THE INFLUENCE OF THE MEDIA

Books

Novelists D. H. Lawrence, William Burroughs, Norman Mailer, and a host of others whose books were once censored, began to dominate the literary scene.

Writers such as Ian Fleming brought to America a new kind of hero—not the clean-cut, truth-telling, sexually unreproachable hero of yesteryear, but the dashing, daring, adventuresome James Bond type. Surrounded by action, violence, and gorgeous and seductive women, Bond made the jobs of daily breadwinning and fidelity to one woman seem incredibly bland.

In 1962 Helen Gurley Brown wrote *Sex and the Single Girl*, deliberately designed to shock and provoke (not to mention sell) with its no-blush instructions on how to carry on an affair. The clear message was "everybody's doing it and you can get in on it, too." Virginity, it seemed, was no longer in vogue.

Magazines

Columnists introduced Hollywood morality into the living rooms of America, even those of families whose convictions prohibited attendance at movies. The phenomenally popular supermarket tabloids—*The National Enquirer* and its clones— capitalized on the nation's growing obsession with sex. Women's magazines, from glamour to romance, became the clearing house for the latest statistics on female orgasm, fantasies, and affairs.

As cagey as an alley cat and almost as moral, Hugh Hefner cashed in on the nation's moral deterioration with *Playboy*. From its inception in 1955, it came on bold and risqué, immersing itself in an illusion of intellectual respectability and journalistic integrity—not an easy task for a technically upgraded form of pornography. Soon *Playboy* was sold in local drugstores alongside candy, gum, and baseball cards. It became as much a part of America as Mom, apple pie, and the girl next door—who was no longer a subject to talk with but an object waiting and wanting to be seduced.

More than a magazine, *Playboy* was a reincarnation of the ancient Epicurean philosophy that elevated personal pleasure over scruples. Playboy window stickers and air fresheners flaunted the bunny, and a whole generation of young men came to believe that women had staples in their navels.

Once it depersonalized sex by shifting the fig leaf to the face, *Playboy* opened the floodgates to a glut of "easy money" soft-porn competitors who made Hefner look like St. Francis in their attempts to outdo each other's raunchiness—of which they repented all the way to the bank. The spread of hard-core pornography took its own toll on the nation's moral fiber, and as we will see in a later chapter, is today a bigger problem than ever.

Motion Pictures

In the fifties and sixties, Hollywood taught American women the art of sexual teasing. Sex symbols such as Marilyn Monroe, Elizabeth Taylor, and Sophia Loren were their tutors. The door they opened to female sexploitation led to later films such as *I am Curious (Yellow)* and *Last Tango in Paris*, where actual intercourse and sexual perversions were shown on the screen.

The motion picture ratings system inspired a glut of "R" movies featuring nudity and sex scenes, yet not branded "X" to avoid the pornographic stigma. Meanwhile the industry that had shocked America with the word "damn" in *Gone With the Wind* soon made profanity and vulgarity chic—almost obligatory.

Television

Television extended the tentacles of the sexual revolution more than any other medium. The early television programs focused on all-American families, such as those in *Father Knows Best*, *Ozzie and Harriet*, and *Leave It to Beaver*. But the sixties' extremely popular *All in the Family* majored in frank discussions not only of racism and bigotry, but of every sexual subject from menopause to impotence to homosexuality. Even the incessant bathroom humor (including the toilet flushing in the background) was a way of saying, "We'll deal with anything on this show—there are no taboos to us." The nation watched each week to see which sacred cows would topple next.

In the sixties, *Peyton Place* brought sexual scandal into America's homes. *Laugh-In* legitimized the dirty joke. *Love American Style* showed how funny adultery could be. The entertainment programs and made-for-TV movies in the late sixties and early seventies paraded a sexual freedom only a few years behind Hollywood. Soon there were sexually exploitive situation comedies like *Soap* and *Three's Company*, and "dramas" like *Charlie's Angels*.

The success of these programs led to the next wave in the seventies and eighties—steamy evening soap operas such as *Dallas* and *Dynasty*. Meanwhile, daytime soap operas, continuing their plunge into voyeurism and vicarious illicit romance, daily shaped the minds and morals of millions. And television's sexual boldness in advertising increased right along with its programming.

The nineties continued the moral decline with sex-saturated programs geared to the young including *Friends*, *Dawson's Creek*, and *Beverly Hills 90210*. *NYPD Blue* pushed the envelope farther, and *Ellen* tried its best to normalize homosexual relations and make it seem like something was wrong with those who didn't think it normal. *Ally McBeal* made lust and sexual fantasies appear amusing and harmless.

Television joined other media in paying homage to celebrities whose performances and personal lives consistently violated Christian morality. As the media assailed the underpinnings of marriage, the divorce rate soared and broken homes multiplied.

Where the Sexual Revolution Left America

The revolution enjoyed one swift victory after another. Filmed and printed erotica that would have shocked in 1965 elicited yawns in 1975. Within less than a decade, the sexual experiments of West Coast college students and hippies became the stuff of everyday life for blue-collar workers in Des Moines and Texarkana. Perhaps never before had such a radical shift in mores occurred in so short a time.[17]

Given the deteriorating spiritual climate of America and the unprecedented potency of the media, the sexual revolution could only succeed. Time allowed a subtle erosion of values and a gradual desensitization to moral changes which, had they come all at once, would never have been tolerated.

In the process of research, it has been fascinating to read the literature of the early and mid 1900s. Some writers warned against the eventual widespread acceptance of fornication, adultery, homosexuality, and abortion on demand. They warned of a self-centered society where personal pleasure was elevated over the corporate good, where pornography and sex crimes flourished and the moral fabric of society was ripped at the seams. Their contemporaries, both secular and Christian, frequently accused them of overreacting. Yet time has proven that these lonely voices, buried in the avalanche of free thinking, were right.

Where was the Church when all this was happening? What did it do to counter the country's moral decline? What is the Church doing today to address the issues of sexual morality and the redemptive needs of sexual sinners? As we will see, the Church's response to the sexual revolution left—and still leaves—much to be desired.

Chapter 2, Notes

1. Pitirim Sorokin, *The American Sex Revolution* (New York: Porter Sargent, 1956), 3-4, 7.

2. For a good historical summary of the Church's perspective on sex, see Letha Scanzoni, *Why Wait?* (Grand Rapids: Baker Book House, 1975), 22-37; and Dwight Harvey Small, *Christian, Celebrate Your Sexuality* (Old Tappan, N.J.: Fleming H. Revell Co., 1974), 46- 101.

3. Scanzoni, *Why Wait?* 35.

4. David Gelman, "Finding the Hidden Freud," *Newsweek,* 30 November 1981,64-70.

5. Steven Marcus, "Devoted to Sex," *New York Times Book Review,* 22 June 1980, 29.

6. Madeline Gray, *Margaret Sanger* (New York: Richard Marek Publishers, 1979), 91.

7. Paul Robinson, *The Modernization of Sex* (New York: Harper and Row, 1976), 4.

8. Dan Gilbert, *The Conspiracy Against Chastity* (San Diego: The Danielle Publishers, 1939), 35.

9. Margaret Sanger, *Pivot of Civilization* (New York: Brentano's, 1922), 282.

10. Elasah Drogin, *Margaret Sanger: Father of Modern Society* (Coarsegold, Calif.: CUL Publications, 1979), 15.

11. Margaret Sanger, "Why Not Birth Control in America?" *Birth Control Review,* May 1919, 10-11.

12. Margaret Sanger, *The Civilizing Force of Birth Control.*

13. Margaret Sanger, *Sex in Civilization,* 532.

14. Quoted in Gilbert, *Conspiracy,* 15.

15. Rollo May, *Love and Will* (New York: W. W. Norton and Co., 1969), 38-39.

16. Joseph Julian and William Kornblum, *Social Problems* (Englewood Cliffs, N.J.: Prentice-Hall, 1983), 78.

17. George Leonard, "The End of Sex," *Esquire,* December 1982, 70.

CHAPTER 3

American Christianity's Response to the Revolution

In its response to the sexual revolution, American Christianity was culpable in at least two areas: it failed to teach a positive and balanced view of sex, and it failed to respond to the revolution with outspoken conviction and courage.

The Christian world, somewhat leery of the secular voices but warm to its own, was led down the path of moral decay by some of its major denominations. Trusted clergymen persuaded significant numbers of lay Christians that Scripture must be updated, reapplied, taken with a grain of salt, or outright denied. Having compromised the teachings of Scripture in an attempt to win an audience, organized religion was left with few listeners and pitifully little to say.

In this tragic display of atrophied conviction and moral cowardice, many (though by no means all) segments of the Church capitulated to the sexual revolution. We have already seen how the grassroots Christian community is riddled with the consequences. Nonetheless, organized Christianity has still not learned from its failures. In its sexual morality the Church is still too often a tail wagged by the dog of the world.

THE CHURCH'S ROLE IN THE REVOLUTION

For the most part, the sexual revolution caught conservative evangelicals and Catholics off guard. They missed an opportunity to clearly affirm a positive view of sex and offer a clear and biblical critique of the culture's decline into immorality. Meanwhile, in 1963 eleven Quakers collaborated to produce *Towards a Quaker View of Sex*. The study justified premarital sex and adultery in certain circumstances and stated that homosexual relations were not sinful per se. The conclusions were particularly significant in that they came from a traditionally conservative religious group.

Mainline Protestant denominations followed with similar theological and moral statements, most of them hedging on or openly rejecting traditional Judeo-Christian sexual values. By 1972, Helen Colton was able to defend a blatantly anti-Christian morality in *Sex After the Sexual Revolution* by quoting rabbis, Catholic priests, and Protestant theologians and ministers.[1]

In some ways, theological liberalism was the sexual revolution's strongest asset. Rather than a light of divine guidance, religion became a mirror of social preference. This is mystifying unless we understand that most of the seminaries that trained church leaders had years before—following society's move to secularism—surrendered their confidence in Scripture. Schools that once raised up apologists for a biblical ethic now produced, at their worst, some of the most effective mouthpieces for the sexual revolution, and at their best, a crop of intellectually astute and biblically illiterate moral milk-toasts.

Here was a strange thing: Christian religion, the revolution's most likely and capable opponent, joining her in an unholy alliance. Even Karl Menninger—named by his peers the greatest living psychiatrist—in *Whatever Became of Sin?* (1973), repeatedly bemoaned the failure of the clergy to courageously call sin, including sexual sin, by its proper name.[2] What could more clearly indicate the dereliction of organized religion than a secular psychologist calling Christian leaders to account for their failure to condemn sin?

Theology Redefines Morality

It was in the fifties and sixties that a new breed of theologians and moralists flexed their muscles in the Church. Some propounded the "God is dead" theology (or nontheology). Many religionists had already concluded "God is distant."

Whether dead or distant, if God was out of the picture, so were the grounds for absolute morality. The Church's attempted dethroning of God also dethroned moral absolutes and their corresponding—and increasingly unpopular—behavioral responsibilities.

Following the logic of philosophers like Alfred North Whitehead and liberal theologian Paul Tillich, Bishop John Robinson's *Honest to God* and *Christian Morals Today* saw the "New Morality" in harmony with the New Testament. Joseph Fletcher made the same defense in his widely read *Situation Ethics*. Many secular spokesmen advocated the same departure from biblical morality as Robinson and Fletcher. What made these men unique, though, was their appeal to the Christian religion itself as the basis for their philosophy. Fletcher made this bold claim of the "New Morality":

> Its roots lie securely, if not conventionally, in the classical tradition of Western Christian morals. It's an old posture with a new and contemporary look.[3]

In a lecture to Southern Baptist leaders (most of whom opposed his views), Fletcher made his position clear:

> I am prepared to argue in the utmost seriousness that Christian obligation calls for lies and adultery and fornication and theft and promise breaking and killing—sometimes, depending upon the situation. And that there is, therefore, negatively expressed, no normative principle of conduct which is universally and unexceptionally obliging, regardless of the relativities and circumstances.[4]

Fletcher went on to say, "each of the so-called Ten Commandments should be amended with the qualifier word 'ordinarily'—for example, the seventh commandment: 'Thou shalt not ordinarily commit adultery.' "

This position was, of course, readily welcomed by millions

of religious Americans who would not ordinarily commit adultery, but found themselves in innumerable extraordinary situations which made it, according to Fletcher, acceptable— perhaps even a matter of Christian obligation.

The popularity of "Situation Ethics" (which became a synonym for the "New Morality") should come as no surprise, given the moral climate of the sixties. Many who wanted to taste the forbidden fruit of immorality were not prepared to directly reject the Christian faith. Now they were told they didn't have to. They could violate biblical standards and in the process still be good Christians.

Progressively outrageous claims began to arise within the Church. In *Honest Sex*, Rustum and Della Roy said the typical American believed that the Bible commanded "premarital chastity" and included a "proscription of adultery." Not so, they said:

> Infinitely better scholars than we have established that one cannot find any literal or simple connection in the Bible claiming that the above . . . were God's law or will.[5]

Defending *Playboy* magazine from the criticisms of "some theologians" (and in the process winning them *Playboy's* endorsement on the book's cover), they claim:

> The death of the old morality has come about without much aid from the Church, but Christians can rejoice at its demise because it has made the way clear for a new approach.[6]

This same morally progressive attitude was reflected in a 1970 document of the United Presbyterian Church of the USA, which stated among other things:

Increasingly, the expectation of premarital virginity is not being met either by men or women. This change is not necessarily to be regarded as a sign of the lowering of the moral standards of young people.[7]

Segments of the Roman Catholic Church have undergone the same moral erosion as liberal Protestantism. For instance, despite—or in reaction to—the Vatican's 1976 condemnation of all extramarital sexual relations, the following year a group of Catholic theologians produced a document defending "creative" sex outside marriage, supporting nonpromiscuous homosexual relationships, denying that bestiality was necessarily pathological, and declaring most pornography to be harmless to adults.[8]

How these religious moral positions differ even slightly from the prevailing secular ones is not apparent. Teaching that the law of God was written in pencil, liberal Christianity thrives on passing out erasers.

Where Is the Church Today?

In June of 1983 the Presbyterian Church (USA) governing body, representing 3.2 million members, voted to accept abortions "within a Christian ethical framework when serious genetic problems arise or when the resources are not adequate to care for a child appropriately."

This decision is significant not just because it allows abortions (so do innumerable groups, secular and religious), but because it does so with *explicit Christian authority*. It is not simply an honest rejection of biblical standards; it is a violation of scriptural principle, not to mention human decency, supposedly rooted in "a Christian ethical framework."

In my book *ProLife Answers to ProChoice Arguments*, I deal with The Religious Coalition for Abortion Rights, who have coined the motto "Prayerfully ProChoice." They have become a powerful ally to abortion advocates precisely because they profess to speak with God's authority. In 1991, a committee appointed by the Presbyterian Church (USA) adopted the most liberal stance imaginable on sex. It could have been mistaken for a tract on free love written in the 1960s instead of a document written by Church people in the 1990s. It advocated "justice love," meaning people could sleep with virtually whomever, whenever they felt like it, provided there was "love." Thankfully, the denomination as a whole voted down this outrageous document. But some have wondered if they did that only because of the negative reaction created by media exposure.

Meanwhile, there are clergy such as Episcopal Bishop John Spong, formerly bishop of Newark, arguing for an end of the traditional Christian prohibitions on sex outside of marriage. He appears on various talk shows wearing the traditional priestly collar and promoting an unbiblical view of sex. He even wrote a book, *Living in Sin?*, which argued that cohabitation is not a sin provided the partners love each other.

It is here that the Church reaches its depths—when it does not simply ignore Scripture in the face of the immoral, but instead uses it, with all its authoritative clout, to *defend* the immoral. At this point the Church becomes a more powerful ally of darkness than the world could ever be. It converts its saints to evil with the very law of God. The Protestant Church in America need not worry about the secular immoralists on the outside; she is being steadily poisoned by the religious immoralists on the inside.

WHAT DOES THE FUTURE HOLD?

Harry Blamires's indictment is most obviously true in the realm of sexual morality:

> The Christian mind has succumbed to the secular drift with a degree of weakness and nervelessness unmatched in Christian history.[9]

Biblical Christianity is an intrinsically and intensely moral religion. Sexual morality is by no means the whole of morality, but it is an important part. The acceptance or endorsement of any immoral practice is ultimately an attack on the faith. More fundamentally, it is an attack on God himself, whose holy character is the basis of biblical morality.

Sexual immorality is a logical corollary to atheism, not Christianity. Its widespread presence and tolerance in the holy Church of Christ is an essential contradiction of what the Church is meant to be.

Two of the seven churches addressed in the book of Revelation are called to account for their tolerance of sexual sin, specifically for permitting some in their midst to promote immortality by their teachings (Revelation 2:14-16; 2:20-23). These kinds of false teachers are prominent in many denominations, seminaries, and churches today. To remove them now that they have become entrenched would be a monumental task . . . but an explicitly biblical one. Christ expected His churches to confront and oppose all immoral teaching in their midst. If they did not, He promised to remove His blessing from the Church.

I am not simply pointing the finger at religious liberals.

The proverbial camel has clearly stuck its nose into the tent of the evangelical Church. If we become content with the presence of the camel's nose, then his head, neck, and forelegs are bound to follow. Left unchecked, the camel of sexual impurity could claim so large a part of the tent that Christian virtue may be unceremoniously pushed out the door. Should that day come—and we are fools if we think it impossible—the words of Jesus will not be, "Well done, thou good and faithful servant," but, "I will remove your lampstand."

Our primary challenge as Christians is not to raise the moral level of the non-Christian world. Our first duty is not to make the world better, but to make the Church better. One thing is certain—an unholy world will never be won to Christ by an unholy Church.

Chapter 3, Notes

1. Helen Colton, *Sex After the Sexual Revolution* (New York: Association Press, 1972), 18-19.

2. Karl Menninger, *Whatever Became of Sin?* (New York: Bantam Books, 1978), 163, 224-25, 231, 236.

3. Joseph Fletcher, *Situation Ethics: The New Morality* (Philadelphia: Westminster Press, 1966), 13.

4. Joseph Fletcher, "Situation Ethics," (Nashville: Christian Life Commission, Southern Baptist Convention, n.d.).

5. Rusturn and Della Roy, *Honest Sex* (New York: Signet, 1972), 68.

6. Ibid., 40-41, 192.

7. Ibid., 5.

8. Anthony Kosnik, ed., *Human Sexuality: New Directions in American Catholic Thought* (New York: Paulist Press, 1977).

9. Harry Blamires, *The Christian Mind* (Ann Arbor, Mich.: Servant Books, 1963), 3.

PART 2

Life in a Technological Corinth

CHAPTER 4

Sex and the Media

Sexual temptations are as old as post-Eden civilization. Twenty-first century America offers no new ones. The old temptations, however, come in sleeker, more colorful packages and are exported as never before to the privacy of the home through mail boxes, air waves, phone lines and modems.

Two thousand years ago the believers in Corinth faced sexual temptation whenever they walked the streets. But today we live in a technological Corinth. We don't have to go out on the streets. Through the wonders of technology, sexual temptation pursues us everywhere. Meanwhile, sin has been given a makeover that hides—but does not change—its ugly face. Thanks to the marvelous media, immorality appears more attractive then ever before.

"Seeing is believing"; "What you see is what you get." Not

so with illusions. Through books, magazines, newspapers, television, movies, music, and computer images our senses are bombarded with a graphic and colorful picture of a vast and enticing sexual world, a world as unreal as it is attractive.

Marshall McLuhan was right when he said years ago,

> All media work us over completely. They are so persuasive in their personal, political, economic, aesthetic, psychological, moral, ethical, and social consequences that they leave no part of us untouched, unaffected, unaltered.[1]

The Media and the Mind

All media touch the mind, stir it, move it, mold it—in every way affect it—even when the process is unconscious. Moreover, the cognitive is basic to the behavioral. We act out what we first think. Hence, whatever affects the mind will ultimately (though not always directly or immediately) affect behavior.

How we think is the reservoir we draw from when we choose how to act. The soundness of our behavior is dependent on the soundness of our thoughts. We are what we think—"As he thinks within himself, so he is" (Proverbs 23:7, NASB).

All behavior, speech as well as actions, begins with thoughts that are formed in the brain using the raw materials sent there by the senses. What do the senses send to the brain? Their impressions of outward stimuli. Hence, the selection of what stimuli—what sights, sounds, smells, tastes, and touches—we expose our senses to dramatically influences the way we eventually think and act.

Furthermore, the brain is not very selective; it records whatever the senses send its way. Like a photographic plate that accumulates light, so the brain accumulates images and impressions. Therefore, what we are today—and what we will be tomorrow—is largely the cumulative product of what we have stored in our brain. And what we have stored there is itself the result of our choices to be stimulated by certain input and not by others.

In the 1950s a respected British newscaster ran a tongue-in-cheek story about the "Annual Spaghetti Harvest." It included films of young women picking armfuls of long pasta hanging from trees, replete with comments about the dreaded "spaghetti weevil." Many Britishers genuinely believed the report, just as many Americans believed Orson Welles's 1938 radio broadcast of "War of the Worlds" and took to the streets to flee the invading Martians.

The point is two-edged: the media are by nature believable, and we are by nature gullible. We learn from birth to be empirical, to believe what we see. Though it is simple for the media to distort, exaggerate, and downright lie, it is not so simple for us to disbelieve them. If television can persuade people about the spaghetti harvest, can't it and other media persuade us to believe falsely about *anything*—whether politics, religion, ethics, or sex?

There is something a bit humorous (and harmless) about an intelligent Britisher going through life believing in the spaghetti weevil. But there is *nothing* funny about people believing that sexual sin is fulfilling, that the best sex is outside marriage, that extramarital sex is really okay, and that the joys of immorality outweigh its consequences. These are, plain and simple, lies. Not harmless jests, like the spaghetti weevil, but *lies*—destructive lies that ruin lives.

We can no longer afford the luxury of naiveté. The influence of the media on our beliefs about sexual morality must be reckoned with.

SEX AND ADVERTISING

No thinking man can consider the force and use of advertising in the modern world without being greatly disturbed.[2]

That most of us are not greatly disturbed about advertising illustrates the point—we're not thinking.

American businesses spend billions of dollars on advertising each year—for prime time television alone. Billions more are spent on daytime television, radio, magazines, newspapers, billboards, and innumerable other media.

There is no free television, no inexpensive magazines. The price we pay is having to look at the commercials and advertisements, which are carefully designed to motivate us—often manipulate us—to spend our money on certain products. Whether the process is conscious or subconscious is immaterial. The fact is, advertising works.

What You're Really Buying

People buy products not for what they are, but for what they are associated with. A man who buys a certain shirt with a certain insignia is buying more than a shirt—he is buying status. He smokes a certain cigarette to be a rugged individualist. He buys a certain beer because he likes to think of himself as an athlete and appreciates close male companionship. His wife buys beauty in the form of soap, his daughter buys male admirers in the form of blue jeans and shampoo. His son buys girlfriends by buying a car. We buy not just products but images.

Of course the images we buy often do not correspond to reality. Who does the beer commercials—alcoholics or athletes? And how often have you seen vomit, lost jobs, crippling car accidents, or broken families in a wine commercial? Look at the virile, healthy people in cigarette ads. How many cigarette ads show people in the oncology ward dying of lung cancer? About as many as show the disastrous side of sex outside marriage. Advertising never lets the truth get in the way of the persuasive goal.

Advertisers know their business better than we know ourselves. They play on our needs and our wants, the most powerful forces in our soul, and they know sex sells.

Sex: The Greatest Tool in Advertising

Why is sex such an effective seller? Because sex is such a powerful drive. It can be associated with a particular product and make that product more appealing. Sex sells everything from cars to toothpaste. When I say sex is an effective seller, I mean subtle, low-key, and playful sexiness. Sex sells best when we barely realize it's there.

From the beginning of the "oldest profession in the world," sex and money have been Siamese twins. In prostitution, sex is sold. In pornography, illusions about sex are sold. In advertising, sex is not sold, but is itself the seller—the tool, the means of sales. It is first the attention getter, then the subtle but effective persuader.

The bottom line motive of big business is not the corruption of morals, but the collection of money. If portraying chastity or premarital virginity and fidelity would sell a product more effectively, they would be used. The first, greatest, and only commandment of corporate advertising is "Sell."

The mind manipulators of Madison Avenue will stop using sex when sex stops selling . . . when you and I stop buying. And, given our sexual natures, drives, and vulnerabilities, that will probably never happen.

The Effects of Advertising's Sexploitation

What is the harm of using sex in advertising? Primarily, I see three negative effects:

1. *The distortion of sexual realities.*

Advertising creates a massive subliminal environment where men and women appear most frequently in fantasy relationships designed to enhance or optimize the mass audience's consuming orientation. We have, of course, made the illusionary media world the real or natural world, permitting the actual material environment to become quite pale, insipid, and ordinary by comparison.[3]

2. *The cultivation and exploitation of human inadequacy.*

Women are carefully trained by media to view themselves as inadequate. They are taught that other women— through the purchases of clothes, cosmetics, food, vocations, avocations, education, etc.—are more desirable and feminine than themselves. Her need to constantly reverify her sexual adequacy through the purchase of merchandise becomes an overwhelming preoccupation, profitable for the merchandisers, but potentially disastrous for the individual.

3. The cultivation of self-centeredness and hedonism.

A commercial for a new automobile tells us "you need this car." We have already been taught to want it—now we are told we need it. Advertising cultivates not the pursuit of holiness but the pursuit of happiness—a happiness wrapped up in material objects and superficial short-term goals.

Meanwhile, we learn a "take what you want" philosophy that applies to sexual morality as well. I may want a car I cannot afford and which, therefore, would be wrong to buy. Or I may want an adulterous relationship which I know is wrong. But when I allow so powerful a force as the media to incessantly tug at my wants, they grow to such proportions that they appear to be needs. Finally, I may succumb and buy the product (the car or the affair), in either case later facing the consequences of my foolishness (far worse for the affair than the car).

Until something is done to reverse mass media sex miseducation, the church's positive witness will have much less impact. The biggest prostitution problem in our country does not come from the bordellos, but from the advertising agencies in business suites where sex fantasies are linked to products in order to increase sales. Consumers share some of the responsibility for such prostitution.[4]

As its Creator, God takes personally this relentless assault upon and abuse of human sexuality. For, ultimately, the exploitation of sex is the exploitation of people, who are sexual beings made in God's image. As Christians, we must refuse to mindlessly submit to this perversion of sex. We must do all in our power to cultivate in ourselves and our families a distaste for and resistance to the exploitation of sex in advertising.

SEX AND THE PRINTED PAGE

"The pen is mightier than the sword." Since Gutenberg, the printing press has become mightier than a million swords. Throughout history the written word has molded minds and morality, and continues to do so today.

A visit to the bookstore is most enlightening. A few years ago I counted thirty-four different books on sex in the new book rack in one Seattle store (this is a respected national chain, not a sleazy adult book store). The "'Sex" department included 109 different books—not just books containing explicit sex (that's in the thousands), but books exclusively devoted to the subject of sex. They ranged from the "How To" manuals to sex lives of famous people, to illustrated histories and instruction manuals in gay and lesbian sex.

As some horrified parents have discovered, many of these books are on public library shelves, and children know where to find them.

Pictureless Pornography

Though laden with sexual overtones, romance novels are not explicit enough for men. Consequently, some publishers specialize in a sort of pictureless pornography that pulls no punches.

Sorokin described the 1950s forerunners of the pulp novels that sell better than ever today:

> The sham literature of our age is designed for the commercial cultivation, propagation, and exploitation of the most degraded forms of behavior. It is pornography that appeals to the basest propensities of that "worst of the beast," as the demoralized human animal was named by Plato and Aristotle. The world of this popular literature is a sort of human zoo, inhabited by raped, mutilated, and murdered females, and by he-males outmatching in bestiality any caveman and outlusting the lustiest of animals; male and female alike are hardened in cynical contempt of human life and values. And what is especially symptomatic is that many of these human animals are made to seem to luxuriate in this way of life, just as, we must assume, the readers enjoy it. This cheap Dante's inferno of aphrodisiacs is painted in the most captivating colors. Instead of exhibiting its filth and rottenness, the pulp-sexualists daze the reader with the glamour of "smartness," "orgasmic" curves, "dynamic" lines, violent passions, and "freedom unlimited" to do anything one wants to do.[5]

By reading only the descriptions on the jacket covers, it is obvious that the books promote sexual perversions of every sort, including swapping, group sex, and incest. The insidious myth that women are asking to be raped, so common in pornography, is likewise prominent in these books:

> Carol knows how to give a man pleasure—her tantalizing body is a rare treasure. She is kidnapped and held for ransom—she doesn't mind, 'cause her abductors are well-built and handsome.

Of course, no one need go to the convenience store for all this literary poison, since even respectable magazines advertise erotic book clubs. Every year, book clubs and booksellers send me and countless others a sale catalog offering innumerable titles, including some featuring nude photos of young girls. All this is sold alongside the great classics, religious works, and Walt Disney children's books.

Most disturbing of all, even the good (i.e., well written) literature is increasingly filled with sex scenes and profane language. Immorality seems almost as obligatory as characters, setting, and plot, even when it's totally unnecessary and out of place. If the glorification of immorality was limited to "the sex books," at least the distinction would be clear. Unfortunately, it is woven into the most popular and influential literature of our day.

Sex and the Magazines

Many men's magazines, even those that aren't pornographic, depend on sex to sell. More alarming still are the detective and police magazines that graphically depict sexual crime, appealing to the reader not only as a voyeur but as a sadist.

Sports magazines are increasingly more explicit in their

photographs. *Sports Illustrated's* annual swimsuit issue is more sexually provocative every year and rivals the *Playboy* of the sixties. Unfortunately, the swimsuit issue also sells twice as many copies as any other issue, reinforcing the publisher's commitment to sexual exploitation and demonstrating that when it comes to sex, it is largely true that the public gets what the public wants.

Among the multitudes of magazines for women, one class in particular specializes in romance. These "confessional" magazines, by frequently employing the word "true" in the titles (e.g., *True Confessions, True Romance*), suggest that women are looking for reality, not just fantasy. The "true" is also incriminating; it tries to convince us that the unbelievable is believable. If the stories were more credible, we wouldn't need to be continually reminded that they are really true.

Through these magazines women are led to drink at an unreal well in an unreal world. How tragic that the lives of many American women are so barren and lonely that they are driven to live vicariously through the atypical and sometimes bizarre, (not to mention unbelievable) experiences of others. Sadder still that their views of reality are thereby warped, and they are drawn always further from the possibility of true personal fulfillment in a relationship.

Another class of women's magazines are the beauty or glamour mags, most of them pervaded with words and images of sex, sexiness, and seduction. *Cosmopolitan* is a glamour magazine that stands out because its editor, Helen Gurley Brown, played a prominent role in the sexual revolution (she wrote the bestselling *Sex and the Single Girl* in 1962).

The famous *Cosmo Report* of 1981 indicated that 68 percent of the readers had committed adultery, and 70 percent over the age of thirty-five had gone to bed with a man on their first date.

A look at the teen magazines shows they follow the pattern of female sexiness, superficiality, and sex-dominated advertising. It is particularly alarming that young female readers are pushed so early into "being sexy."

Millions of American minds are touched weekly through the supermarket tabloids. These are the newspapers with three inch headlines that typically read, NUDE GHOSTS OF ELVIS AND JFK DESCEND FROM UFO AND GIVE MADONNA MIRACULOUS HERB THAT CURES ARTHRITIS. Actual titles include "Hitler's Sex Life," "Sex Confessions of Daytime Superstuds," and "Love Secrets of Soaps Bitches." The lead caption of the latter article reads:

> Daytime TV's two superbitches are the secret envy of millions of American women because they get to go to bed with men who are not their husbands.[6]

The large number of Christian products and services advertised in these sensational tabloids indicates a significant readership of professing Christians. Out of 134 classifieds looking for love in one issue, thirteen specifically state they are born-again Christians; others would likely say the same. A typical one reads:

> Christian divorced lady, 34, considered very attractive, TV star type, long blond hair, seeks correspondence with honest, Christian male. Only Christians need reply. Photo please.

That professing believers, and no doubt some are genuine ones, would regularly read material that majors in sensationalism, trivia, and shabby reporting is disturbing enough. That they would read material that glorifies the occult, astrology, materialism, and sexual immorality is even more disturbing.

SEX AND TELEVISION

Promise me you'll read this section even if you have to miss your favorite TV show. The odds are against me.

More U.S. homes have television than indoor plumbing Ninety-eight percent have one TV, many have two, three, or more. Considering that fifty years ago no one had any, the television has rapidly assumed a remarkable role in American life.

The average home's TV is on seven hours every day.[7] Many Americans spend more time watching television than working. The average child two to five years old spends one-third of his waking hours watching television. A teenager has spent fifteen thousand hours watching TV by the time he graduates, three thousand more hours than the time spent in school. If the typical young American lives to be seventy, he will have spent ten full years—of twenty-four hour days—in front of the television.

No matter who says what about the effects of television or the mind and behavior, one thing is clear—it is impossible to spend that much time doing anything without being permanently affected by it.

The Minds and Morals Behind Television

Television is not just a seller of products to human minds, it is itself a product of human minds. *Public Opinion* reports that of 104 influential television writers, producers, and executives,

80 percent did not regard homosexual relations as wrong, 51 percent did not think adultery was wrong (only 17 percent felt strongly that it was wrong), and 97 percent favored a woman's right to have an abortion.

These statistics are far more liberal than that of the rest of American society. "According to television's creators, they are not in it just for the money. They also seek to move their audience toward their own vision of the good society."[8]

A team of Michigan State researchers studied television's soap operas and noted that in addition to continuous allusions to sex, the average soap includes two "intimate sexual acts" per hour. More significantly, however, it found that "94% of all daytime copulations, if rape and prostitution are included, occur between unmarrieds." Obviously, this is a gross distortion of real life, where most sexual relations are between those married (to each other). But by sheer percentages it overwhelms viewers with the commonness and acceptability of fornication and adultery.

If television is to be believed, the wages of sin is not always death, you may or may not reap what you sow, God is nonexistent or irrelevant, problems are quickly and cheaply solved (always within thirty or sixty minutes), committed Christians are hypocrites and bigots, and only the ignorant, uptight, and unattractive confine their sexual activity to marriage.

One hundred million Americans go to church regularly. How many television characters go to church? How many pray, read the Bible, and live by biblical morality? Why don't they? Because the writers and producers don't. What they write and produce reflects their values, which are far afield, not only of believers, but of most of the country.

The moral gap between the media elite and the rest of society will not last long, of course. In time, most of us will think as they do now (just as we now think as they did fifteen years ago). Jesus said it this way: "Everyone who is fully trained will be like his teacher" (Luke 6:40). For hours on end, Americans young and old, sit at the feet of their media mentors.

Programming Content

Television offers an endless smorgasbord of brawl chases, shootings, stabbings, rapes, and murders of every variety. Prime time is crime time. The average child will see on television twenty thousand acts of violence by the time he is eighteen. Given the glut of situation comedies, dramas, and made-for-television movies with sexually suggestive, often sexually explicit, dialogue and scenes, who knows how many acts of immorality he will see. Says one producer, "Titillation always sells."[10]

I remember some years ago, the much-heralded episode of the television program *Doogie Howser*, where the title character was going to solve his big "problem." His big problem was his virginity, and he was going to go out and lose it. Tragically, they presented this in a very inviting way—with seductive music, good lighting, and slow motion moves. At the time, this was one of the highest rated television programs. They presented it as if Doogie Howser was finally going to become a man, as if losing one's virginity were somehow a sign of manhood. For many, television is their chief sex educator. The problem is that it usually teaches the wrong lessons.

Sex on Cable and Pay TV

During my study of network television, I bought a programming guide that listed the other shows I could have watched in that same two-day period if I subscribed to a cable service, HBO, and Showtime. The endless barrage of violent and immoral movies made the network fare, itself offensive to any thinking person, seem almost tame by comparison.

I find it interesting—and revealing—that many Christian families pay to have these movie channels in their homes. Admittedly, some of the programming is good, and you don't have to watch the bad stuff. But I wouldn't buy subscriptions to ten raunchy men's magazines in order to get three or four good ones, would you? Maybe I wouldn't trust myself—or my children—to keep away from the bad ones. If I was morally strong at the moment I could throw away the bad magazines when they came in the mail, but I can't do that with a television. It just sits there, waiting to be turned on at any point of boredom, curiosity, or moral weakness. Maybe I can resist temptation this time, but the same movie plays again tomorrow night, when the family's gone. . . .

I also don't like the idea of paying for something (even if I don't watch it) which so obviously violates the Word of God and dishonors His holy character.

SEX AND THE MOVIES

Video cassette players have provided the first direct link between Hollywood and the home. Everything that's in movie theaters—and much more—is in the video store. Christian adults and children routinely wander the aisles looking at explicit sexual imagery on the video boxes.

It's interesting how many movies in the "comedy" section are saturated with sex.

Laughter can be wonderful, but it is far more serious than we might think. What I laugh at makes a statement about my values. I don't laugh at that which violates deep-seated convictions. If something entertains me, it must in some sense be acceptable to me.

The media excels at prompting Americans to laugh at immorality—thereby gradually but effectively lowering our moral standards. And no medium has entertained us with immorality so effectively as the motion pictures.

I'm going to use an illustration now that I hope makes you very uncomfortable. It does me. Suppose I came to you and said, "There's an attractive girl down the street. Let's get together and go look through her window and watch her undress and lay back on a couch and pose naked from the waist up. Then this girl and her boyfriend will go get in a car and have sex—let's get as close as we can and listen to them and watch the windows steam up."

You'd be shocked. Your respect for me would dissolve. You'd think, "he's disqualified for the ministry." And you'd be absolutely right.

Suppose I then said, "Listen, the young woman has given us permission. She knows we'll be looking at her. She doesn't mind." Would that change your thinking about the situation? Of course not.

But suppose, instead, I invited you over to my house and said, "Let's watch *Titanic*."

The majority of Christians have seen this movie, many recommend it, whole youth groups view it together, and many have purchased it and show it in their homes.

Instead of looking through a window glass, they look through a television glass. But they still watch people undress and seduce each other and have sex together. They never seem to ask how something shameful somehow becomes moral because it's watched through one kind of glass instead of another.

"*Titanic*? Wonderful. It wasn't even rated R!" This was one committed Christian's assessment of the movie.

Suppose I said to you, "My wife and I are going to make love tonight. Why don't you come over and watch? And when we're done, we'll watch you and your wife have sex. It's okay, we're married."

How would you react? Well, what if instead I said, "Let's watch *Braveheart*"?

Think about it. Every day Christians across the country, including many church leaders, watch women and men undress through the window of television and watch people commit acts of fornication and adultery that our God calls an abomination. That's what it is—that's the truth. And that's how out of touch with the truth we've become. We're a bunch of voyeurs, peeping toms, entertained by sin.

There's nothing new about sexual immorality. But there's something new about the ease with which it invades our home. Christians who wouldn't consider going to a strip club watch strippers on videos, TV shows and even news programs. Parents who wouldn't dream of letting a dirty-minded adult alone with their children do that very thing every time they let their kids sit and surf channels without supervision.

THE EFFECTS OF TELEVISION AND MOVIES

Do television and motion pictures *really* affect our lives? Absolutely.

The proliferation of sex-saturated programs and movies has created a nation of voyeurs. And voyeurism is a sexual sickness, whether done through binoculars, window shades, peepholes, or in living rooms and movie theaters. It is a symptom of sexual sickness and bondage, not sexual health and freedom.

Moreover, many motion pictures are targeted for the young—those whose sexual identities and values are still being shaped and who will determine the moral direction of our country.

Television affects our sleeping habits, our eating habits, and even our bathroom habits.[11] Passivity, consumption of alcohol, and obesity are all promoted by television. Think of those endless hours of gazing lifelessly with nothing to do but eat, drink, and watch commercials about eating and drinking.

In addition to these more obvious influences, television and the movies have introduced other serious negative effects into our national psyche.

1. *Television and movies cultivate unhealthy cross-sexual relationships.*

After his thorough training to view women as sex objects, the media-oriented young American male finds it most difficult to relate or interact with women as human beings. . . .

Every large American city has tens of thousands of working women—many highly talented, sensitive, and interesting women—who are unlikely to establish permanent mates because they physically do not fit into the current media-induced fantasy of what an attractive woman should look like.[12]

2. *Television and movies promote inadequacy, insecurity, and superficiality.*

Every time I meet a slender twenty-year-old girl who constantly exercises and starves herself, yet feels she must lose fifteen pounds, I get angry at the media. The epidemic of anorexia and bulimia is largely attributable to the "emaciated is beautiful" message American women (especially the young) are given from every program, movie, magazine, billboard, and store mannequin. Many, both male and female, are preoccupied with the superficial and trendy to the neglect of character and moral fiber.

3. *Television and movies promote immorality and crime, both sexual and violent.*

Some criminals have specifically stated that many of their ideas and techniques for crime came from television (often while they were watching in prison, prior to parole).

At least fifteen people committed suicide imitating a Russian roulette scene in *Deerhunter*, a popular movie shown on television. John Hinckley got his idea of stalking the president from the movie *Taxi Driver*, which he watched fifteen times. A nineteen-year-old boy watched the television movie *Lizzie Borden*, then killed his parents and sister and crippled his brother with an axe.

Violent rapes, murders, and crimes of every sort are common fare in the media. Is it any wonder that violent crimes increased so dramatically in the sixties, the very decade where television entrenched itself as the center of America's attention?

4. *Television and movies desensitize viewers, especially children,*
to human dignity and needs and make them more callous to
human suffering.

Even the news often focuses on grisly killings and sex slay-
ings. But merely by watching prime time programs (even some
cartoons), children are constantly bombarded with violence
and immorality, putting tremendous adult pressures on them
at far too young an age. What does it do to the psychosexual
development of a prepubescent girl when she continually
watches women seducing and propositioning men on television? Young men watching *Titantic* are tempted toward lust,
and young women are tempted toward believing that the way
to relate to a man is to behave seductively.

How many murders and seductions did your grandparents
see as children? Probably a grand total of none. How about
you? It depends on your age and whether or not you had a
television when you were young. Now how many murders
and seductions have your children seen? Hundreds—most of
them thousands.

What is premarital sex to a teenager who has seen it on
television ever since he was a preschooler? Upon finding he
has fathered a child as a sixteen-year-old, why do his parents
throw up their hands and cry, "God, where did we go wrong?"
What's the big mystery? Through the media he's been taught
daily since childhood that sex outside of marriage is not only
okay, but fun, exciting, perfectly normal, and generally free of
consequences.

Do we really think that occasional moral sermons from
parents or youth pastors can counteract the cumulative exposure of the thousands of hours of slick media tutorials that
have discipled our children to believe the opposite? Why

should we expect them to do anything but violate God's sexual standards when they have for so long seen it done in such grand and engaging style?

And while we're asking the tough questions, whose fault is it that the television we used as our child's babysitter turned out to be his kidnapper? You won't find it in the books, but television may be one of the most serious forms of child abuse in this country.

Part of that child abuse takes place on the Internet, where kids have so much easy access to sexual exploitation. Some children encounter child molesters (without recognizing them as such) on chat rooms; more often, they get exposed to sexual images they can never erase.

Donna Rice Hughes wrote a book, *Kids On-line: Protecting Your Children in Cyberspace.* In an interview, she warned parents about the dangers the Internet poses to their children:

> With unrestricted Internet access, it's very easy for anyone, including a child, to come across all kinds of pornography. They can come across it intentionally by simply typing a word such as "sex" into a search engine. That will deliver many pornographic sites on the world-wide web. But the real problem is that children can get this material unintentionally . . . . A child could innocently type, for instance, "boys," into a search engine. They could come across some really great sites about boys, but they could also come across hard-core pornography sites. The same with "toys."

SUMMARY

Fellow Christians have often recommended a particular television program, assuring us "there's nothing offensive about it." Frequently we have followed their advice and turned on the program only to have to turn it off again within the first ten minutes. The content is often subtly and sometimes blatantly immoral.

Why didn't these sincere Christians see what appeared so obvious? Why didn't they see the glaring inconsistency of the program with their biblical values? For the same reason *we* would no longer see it if we chose to go on watching such programs. Desensitization of the conscience is as predictable as it is potent. The more we expose ourselves to morally offensive input, the less offensive it becomes to us. Our moral sensitivities are dulled. Eventually we are neither offended ourselves nor do we understand why others are. I confess that I, too, am more desensitized than in the past. While my standards are higher than most, I tolerate things on television and in movies I once would not have. This causes me concern. If I don't do something about it, what will I be tolerating in five years that I don't now? Where will it stop?

It is the height of ignorance to think that any person, young or old, Christian or non-Christian, could read the literature and watch the programs and movies described in this chapter and remain in any sense personally and morally unscathed.

A college freshman, born and raised in a strong Christian family and active in our church youth group, told me of an explicit sexual movie he had seen the night before. (This was not a confession or admission, just a matter of fact that arose in our conversation.)

"How did it affect you?" I asked.

He paused. "I don't know, actually. I didn't really think about it. I don't think most people do."

And that is the tragedy. A mind is molded most completely not when it thinks, but when it doesn't think. A Christian who thinks would fare much better seeing such movies. But a Christian who thinks would never watch them in the first place.

Unthinkingly, without measuring, filtering, or processing, we expose our minds to that which, were we thinking, would be unthinkable. And each time—gradually, subtly, imperceptibly—we surrender just a little more mental and moral turf to anti-Christian values. Our circle of holiness shrinks a smidgen more, and the hard-fought gains from spiritual disciplines, meditation, and prayer dissipate until one day we wake up morally bankrupt. . . or we do not wake up at all.

Chapter 4, Notes

1. Marshall McLuhan and Quentin Fiore, *The Medium Is the Message* (New York: Random House, 1967), 26.

2. Harry Blamires, *The Christian Mind* (Ann Arbor, Mich.: Servant Books, 1963), 28.

3. Wilson Bryan Key, *Media Sexploitation* (Englewood Cliffs, N.J.: Prentice-Hall, 1976), 20-21.

4. Ibid., 19.

5. Pitirim Sorokin, *The American Sexual Revolution* (New York: Porter Sargent, 1956), 24-25.

6. The *National Examiner*, 31 May 1983, 1.

7. *USA Today*, 17 April 1984, sec. D.

8. "TV Executives Differ Sharply from the Public on Moral Beliefs," *Christianity Today*, 8 April 1983, 56-57.

9. Rebekkah Bricker and Carolyn Dykhouse, "Do Skin and Sin on the Soaps Affect Viewers?" *People*, 14 June 1982, 76.

10. *USA Today*, 30 August 1984, sec. D

11. City water systems dramatically drop their water pressure when toilets are flushed during prime time commercials (Gregg Lewis, *Telegarbage* [Nashville: Thomas Nelson Publishers, 1977], 24).

12. Key, *Media Sexploitation*, 18, 60.

CHAPTER 5

Pornography and Other Sex Crimes

Americans spend approximately $12-13 billion per year on pornography.[1] This includes pornographic videos, magazines, and phone sex. Laurie Hall, author of *An Affair of the Mind*, points out: "That's more money than if you combined the annual revenues of the Coca-Cola and the McDonnell Douglas corporations."[2]

In the early fifties, stores carried no soft pornography. In the sixties *Playboy* established a firm position "behind the counter." In the seventies, *Penthouse* took its place beside *Playboy*. Now, at three local convenience stores in my rural area, the average is twelve behind-the-counter magazines.

What Is Pornography?

Pornography may be defined as any visual, written, or recorded stimulus designed to cultivate or heighten a person's desire toward immoral sexual behavior. Not every mention of immorality is pornographic. The Bible often talks about immorality, but always with the purpose of deterring the reader from it, not attracting him to it.

Pornography is increasingly characterized by extreme sexual violence. Sadomasochism—with its violence—is common fare in hard porn magazines. Lonely and disturbed men consume pornography like saltwater, gorging themselves to the point of sickness and despair. Always craving more, they require new depths of depravity to stimulate them, depths so violent and grotesque I dare not record them. The pornographic world is a world of nightmares that defies belief.

Knowing the Christian faith is their greatest potential enemy, pornographers often attack it. *Playboy* carried an article that mocked Christ's virgin birth, rewriting it in modern terms as a cheap sexual seduction of God by Mary, in league with her husband, because they wanted a baby of high intelligence. *Hustler* and *Screw* magazine have gone even further, displaying a naked woman on the cross and depicting not only Christian leaders, but Jesus Christ Himself, in sexual perversions.

Defending the Indefensible

Given pornography's true nature, it's incredible that it is sometimes called a "victimless crime." Nothing could be further from the truth. The subjects photographed are one kind of victim, those they portray another, and the viewer—sucked ever more deeply into the black hole of lust—yet another. Those against whom the pornography addict acts out his aggressions are the ultimate victims, as are their families and society as a whole. Whether obvious or subtle, pornography *thrives* on victims.

Despite all this, numerous books, articles, and commission reports have gone to great lengths to defend pornography.

Most often it is defended by the First Amendment: "Congress shall make no law . . . abridging the freedom of speech, or of the press. . . ." Who knows how many millions of dollars the American Civil Liberties Union (ACLU) has poured into their relentless efforts to hide pornography behind the Constitution?

Postal authorities exercised their legal responsibility to hand over to the FBI the names of people importing large amounts of illegal child pornography from Scandinavia. The ACLU was outraged. After all, the rights of these citizens were being violated! Yet these self-proclaimed freedom defenders seem not at all outraged at the exploited, raped, and murdered children whose civil liberties, human dignity, and lives are robbed by the very people they defend. As a result of the ACLU's efforts, freedom rings the cash registers of organized crime.

That free speech and press are not absolute is demonstrated by the old observation: "No one has a right to [falsely] shout 'Fire' in a crowded theater." Likewise, no one has the right to print or speak lies about others or to plagiarize their work. The First Amendment is not and has never been an unqualified license to say or print whatever anyone wants. It was intended to protect a free and decent society, not to make the unprincipled wealthy as they prey upon the weak.

"Expert witnesses" (professionals flown in by—who else?—the ACLU) often testify at obscenity trials that pornography isn't really obscene or that obscenity is a constitutional right. They top off their argument with the kind of quantum-leap logic that goes like this: "If we let them ban *Teen Slut* today, they'll be burning the Mona Lisa tomorrow." A similar line of thinking is that if drunk drivers are given suspended licenses, the next thing we know they'll take away all our cars.

Pornographers and their defenders often make their cases by finding a token passage or picture that is "socially redeeming." Similarly, restaurant owners threatened with closure by a health inspector might attempt to justify their right to serve food by pointing to an edible carrot amongst the spoiled, moldy, and disease-ridden offerings of their salad bar.

Another favorite defense of pornography is the idea that sexual activity is a reality, and there is no justification for censoring anything real. Measured by Christian morality, what is real and what is right are often galaxies apart. But the truth is that what pornography conveys is not real. Pornography doesn't tell the truth; it lies about sex. Pornography portrays human bodies with proportions that are not the norm. It depicts sex in freakish, bizarre, and grotesque manners. It states or implies that women are asking to be raped and that children are seductive. Pornography lies in a thousand ways. Pornography is real; what it portrays is not.

Pornography is trash precisely because it treats people as trash. It is antiwomen, antichildren, antihuman, and anti-God, in whose image its victims are made.

The pornography industry thrives because greedy people

want the money of lustful people, and ignorant or indifferent people do nothing to stop it.

Theories about Pornography's Effects

The greatest blow to antipornography efforts in modern history was the Presidential Commission on Obscenity and Pornography created in January 1968. After two years and two million dollars, the Commission concluded that there was no cause-effect relationship between pornography and violence. Pornography was declared essentially harmless.[3]

The president and U.S. Senate rejected the findings of the report. The Commission not only failed to use common sense, but ignored much of the evidence. This should have come as no surprise, since most of the Commission members were solidly anticensorship. Incredibly, those responsible chose as chairman of the Commission an active leader of the ACLU, an action akin to asking an executive of the American Tobacco Growers to chair a commission to determine whether smoking can harm your health. Subsequent pornography commissions have included more conscientious evaluators, including Dr. James Dobson of Focus on the Family, an outspoken advocate of sexual morality.

There are many different theories about the effects of pornography. One is simply that there are no effects. This position displays gross ignorance of the human mind, the persuasive power of visualization, the relation of the cognitive to the behavioral, and the inherent power of the sex drives.

Another theory is that viewing pornography is a catharsis —a harmless outlet that actually reduces aggressive and violent behavior. Presumably thought up by a research team sponsored by organized crime, this theory is preposterous. It not only goes against all the scientific data, but flies in the face of experience as well.

Similar to the concept of catharsis is the boredom theory—the idea that the more pornography is available, the more commonplace and boring it becomes, and therefore, the less it will be craved. This is a dangerous half-truth. Scientific tests do show that prolonged exposure to pornography lessens sexual stimulation. Boredom *does* set in, often after there has been a sexual release. But temporary boredom or release does not change the important fact that the pornography *addict* always comes back for more. A chocolate addict, given a ten-pound Hershey bar, may devour it, get sick, and not want chocolate for a day or two, but he will come back more hooked than ever, wanting and needing more.

Increased exposure does not lead to indifference but to desensitization, which produces a craving for more potent and destructive stimulation. It is true of drugs and alcohol, and just as true of pornography. It is this ongoing cycle of addiction and desensitization and further addiction and desensitization that demands new depths in sexual perversions. The old turnons don't work anymore. No wonder that in 1970 the typical cover of a pornographic magazine was of a woman posing alone. By 1983 a survey of seventeen hundred pornographic magazines showed that nine out of ten covers depicted scenes of bondage and domination. The deeper someone gets into pornography, the deeper his tastes and demands for the worst of perversions.

The Truth about Pornography's Effects

The no-effect, catharsis, and boredom theories are wrong. The only view that fits reality is that pornography has significant effects on sexual attitudes, perceptions, drives, morals, behavior, and interpersonal (especially cross-sexual) relationships. London University professor H. J. Eysenck declared:

> It cannot any longer be argued with any degree of conviction that pornography, or the portrayal of violence, has no effect on the behavior of the people who see these things on the screen, or read about them in books or magazines. . . . Both behavior and emotional reactions are affected and the effects are not transitory.[4]

Eysenck coauthored *Sex, Violence and the Media*, a scientific collection of data, carefully accumulated and evaluated. He concluded that without a doubt pornography measurably increases one's tolerance of and inclination toward acts of violence, including rape.[5]

Victor Cline reached the same conclusion in an excellent collection of articles on pornography in *Where Do You Draw the Line?*[6] Cline's research affirms that pornography is addicting, desensitizing, and escalating, and that it pushes its users to act out what they see. Similarly, Edward Donnerstein of the University of Wisconsin and Neil Malamuth of UCLA say their research "has shown conclusively that viewing violence—especially sexual assault—has notably spurred male viewers to violent acts toward women."[7]

Police vice squads report that more than three-fourths of child molesters admit they have imitated sexual behavior they have seen in pornography. In the state of Michigan, of thirty-eight thousand reported sexual assault cases, 41 percent involved the use of pornography "just prior to or during the crime."[8] I have in front of me eight newspaper clippings about sexual crimes which specifically mention the criminal's addiction to pornography. Neil Gallagher cites many case histories of hideous crimes, including rape, sodomy, sex torture, and murder, directly linked to viewing pornography.[9]

A Christian View of Pornography?

I am concerned that some Christians leaders are underestimating the seriousness of viewing pornography. A Netherlands pastor states:

> Surely the Christian will be moved more by the human sadness that helps create the pornography market than by his own distaste for the product. There is also the possibility that pornography will lose its appeal once it is on the free and open market for a time. *It is no sin to look at pornography;* but only sadness and frustration can keep people looking at it for long [italics mine].[10]

"Distaste for the product" implies a matter of personal preference—as if the issue was not clear-cut. More troubling is the suggestion that unrestrained distribution of pornography may help the problem. Narcotics are easier than ever to obtain, and the result is a bigger problem, not smaller.

Most striking, however, is the categorical statement that looking at pornography is not a sin. Is it *never* a sin? Doesn't pornography stimulate to lust? Didn't Jesus say lust was sin? Isn't it sinful to choose to be stimulated to lust?

Note the logic in this quote from an American evangelical seminary professor:

Is the person who gets excited by sexually stimulating photographs lusting? The answer must be that it all depends. An adolescent paging through a *Playboy* magazine may be doing more than satisfying his curiosity; but he's not necessarily lusting after those faceless figures of centerfold land. The husband who is distracted, tired, depressed and in general out of tune with his own sexuality, may feel the need of a sexual stimulus that his wife, unfortunately, does not provide. If he sneaks a look at some touched-up picture of an undressed woman, he may, in fact, be merely receiving the stimulus he needs to make love to his wife. Now it may be sad that some men or women need this kind of stimulus; their spouses may have reason to put more life into their own sexual style. But in this real world of pressures and distractions, any person who insists on being the only sexual stimulus in the world for his/her spouse is courting disillusionment.[11]

What this author sees as sad is certainly that, but isn't it also sin? And isn't there a message here that indulging in a little pornography on the side won't really hurt anything? That maybe it can even *help* by rekindling attraction to one's spouse?

I have seen men who once, then repeatedly "sneak a look" at pornography and are drawn toward adultery. Often they lose their sexual attraction to the one woman God has given them to enjoy sex with. I have also seen the low self-esteem of real women who have lost their husbands to the fantasy nymphs of *Playboy* and Hollywood; who see themselves compared to abnormal female physiques with which they cannot compete. As their husband's sex partner, they feel second-rate and inferior, and their own enjoyment of sex is nil. Dehumanized, degraded, and demoralized, they too are victims of the victimless crime.

The world supplies us with plenty of ammunition to rationalize lust and defend pornography. We don't need any more from the Church.

The Pornography-Prostitution-Rape Link

Pornography is related to two other crimes: prostitution and rape. I speak of "crimes" in a moral, not a legal sense. Much pornography is legal, even some prostitution is legal, and most abortion is legal. Yet morally, they are all crimes.

Prostitution is the selling of one's body for use in sexual activities. It is a major problem in most cities and is often tied to organized crime, drug abuse, pornography, and illegal activities of every sort.

Prostitutes are both female and male. Most of the women are young, and almost all the males are boys. The customers of both are invariably men. Winked at by society and all too often glorified by the media, prostitution is given a sugarcoated appearance that belies the horrible human exploitation at its base.

The crime of rape occurs with frightening regularity.

It is often stressed that rape is a crime of violence, not sex. I don't believe this is entirely true. Though certainly a crime of violence, we should not underestimate the role of sex in the question of how and why the rapist has come to hate and seek vengeance upon women. Often it is a result of prolonged exposure to women as inhuman sex objects—as teases, deserving or wanting to be raped.

The marked increase of rape is directly linked, I believe, to the dehumanization of women fostered not only by the fantasies of pornography, but by those of the respected media. We have no reason to believe that rape will decrease as long as minds are exposed to sexual myths about women and children and as long as the legal system treats rape as less than a most serious offense. Rape should result, minimally, in long imprisonment without parole. Release should be made only when there is significant evidence that the criminal will not repeat the crime.

So many rapists are released because of insufficient evidence (their word against the woman's), and so many are paroled even if they are convicted, that many women fear revenge if they turn them in. Add to this the personal humiliation rape victims are dragged through (sometimes) by the police and (often) by defense attorneys and the media, and it is no wonder that nine out of ten rapes are never reported.

Rape victims experience wide ranges of personal trauma, including fear, guilt, insecurity, loss of self-respect, and loss of trust, as well as physical symptoms such as headaches, stomach pain, and insomnia (pregnancies by rape sometimes, though rarely, occur). An excellent book for rape victims and those ministering to them is *Raped*, by Deborah Roberts.[12]

There are countries in which rape is virtually nonexistent. Ours, however, has fostered a sex-saturated climate in which sexual distortions flourish and, therefore, rape thrives. Only by making fundamental changes in our sexual mores will we be able to help American women and children again be safe on their streets and in their homes.

Chapter 5, Notes

1. Randy Frame, "Pornography: Once More into the Trenches," *Christianity Today*, 4 March 1983, 73.

2. *Presidential Commission Report on Obscenity and Pornography* (New York: Bantam, 1970).

3. Neil Gallagher, *The Porno Plague* (Minneapolis, Minn.: Bethany House Publishers, 1981),14-15.

4. Quoted in John H. Court, *Pornography: A Christian Critique* (Downers Grove, Ill.: InterVarsity Press, 1980), 78.

5. H. J. Eysenck and D. K. B. Nias, *Sex, Violence and the Media* (New York: St. Marin's Press, 1978).

6. Victor B. Cline, "Comments and Conclusions," in *Where Do You Draw the Line?* ed. Victor B. Cline (Provo, Utah: Brigham Young University Press, 1974), 343-58.

7. *The National Decency Reporter*, May-June 1983, 3.

8. Harry Genet, "Why People Don't Fight Porn," *Christianity Today*, 1 January 1982, 52.

9. Gallagher, *Porno Plague*, 19-25.

10. J. Rinzema, *The Sexual Revolution* (Grand Rapids, Mich.: Wm. B. Eerdmans Publishing Co., 1974), 104.

11. Lewis B. Smedes, *Sex for Christians* (Grand Rapids, Mich.: Wm. B. Eerdmans Publishing Co., 1976), 211-12.

12. Deborah Roberts, *Raped* (Grand Rapids, Mich.: Zondervan Publishing House, 1981).

CHAPTER 6

Backlash to the Great Sex Swindle

Lenina shook her head. "Somehow," she mused, "I haven't been feeling very keen on promiscuity lately. There are times when one doesn't. Haven't you found that too, Fanny?"

Fanny nodded her sympathy and understanding. "But one's got to make the effort," she said sententiously, "one's got to play the game. After all, everyone belongs to everyone else."

"Yes, everyone belongs to everyone else," Lenina repeated slowly and, sighing, was silent for a moment: then, taking Fanny's hand, gave it a little squeeze. "You're quite right, Fanny. As usual, I'll make the effort."

This dialogue from Aldous Huxley's *Brave New World* illustrates what happens to sex when it is ripped from the protective moorings of marriage. It becomes bland, boring, empty, and meaningless. It leaves one wondering what it was that used to seem so great about sex. And that is precisely what has happened in our own brave new world. By 1980 people were beginning to realize this sexual revolution was a dead-end street.

Many people are now beginning to question the joys of "sex." A September 1980 *Cosmopolitan* magazine survey of more than 106,000 women showed that a revolution had indeed taken place in sexual behavior, as well as in attitude. But a majority of the women surveyed indicated their disillusionment and disappointment with "the emotional fruit the sexual revolution has borne." According to the *Cosmopolitan* report, "So many readers wrote negatively about the sexual revolution, expressing longings for vanished intimacy, and the now elusive joys of romance and commitment, that we've begun to sense that there might be a sexual counterrevolution underway in America."[1]

Discovering the Hidden Costs of Free Sex

In 1969, at the early fever pitch of the sexual revolution, psychotherapist Rollo May wrote *Love and Will*, called by the *New York Times* "the most important book of the year." Right as the sexual revolution was rising to a pitch, May stated:

By anesthetizing feeling in order to perform better, by employing sex as a tool to prove prowess and identity, by using sensuality to hide sensitivity, we have emasculated sex and left it vapid and empty. The banalization of sex is well-aided and abetted by our mass communication. For the plethora of books on sex and love which flood the market have one thing in common—they oversimplify love and sex, treating the topic like a combination of learning to play tennis and buying life insurance. In this process, we have robbed sex of its power.[2]

George Leonard, once a strong proponent of the sexual revolution, would have taken issue with May in 1969. By 1982, however, he had changed his tune:

As for "sex," it has become something you "have." You have a car, you have dinner, you have a swim, you have the chickenpox . . . and you have sex. . . .

Casual recreational sex is hardly a feast—not even a good, hearty sandwich. It is a diet of fast foods served in plastic containers. . . . Indiscriminate, obligatory "getting-it-on" is losing its charm. The best-kept secret of the sexual revolution is at last coming out of the closet; what people want most of all (though sometimes they can hardly bear to say it) is a return to the personal in all things—especially in erotic love.[3]

Author of *The End of Sex*, Leonard coined the expression "high monogamy"—his term for the radical idea of the lifelong commitment of two partners to "erotic exclusivity," sex only with each other. (Sounds suspiciously like marriage, doesn't it?)

Writing in *New York* magazine, Fran Schumer quotes a veteran of the sexual revolution:

"It doesn't surprise anyone when you say 'Good night' these days," she says. "People aren't interested in sex. They'd rather have someone they can see than someone they don't want to face the next day because they went to bed with them prematurely."

This is not the kind of frank admission anyone could have made ten years ago, when the sexual revolution was just hitting its stride. That movement appears to have moved ahead in its life cycle. People are saying "No" more and sleeping around less. The one-night stand has lost a measure of allure: in its stead are relationships. Words like "commitment" and "responsibility" command new respect, as do "intimacy" and "love." Its stormy adolescence behind it, a movement spawned in reaction to '50s taboos is now heading placidly to middle age. . . .

Indeed, a generation that skipped the hand-holding stage of adolescence is rediscovering dating. There's romance instead of lust, courtship in place of seduction. Pushed into the closet by the revolution, virginity has pushed its way back out.[4]

Why this rash of sexual conservativism? Boredom may be part of it. But many people are not just bored; they are hurt. They view the revolution with a jaundiced eye. They see it as a Trojan horse that promised treasure while it bootlegged in disaster. They're victims of a great sex rip-off—and they resent it.

Where Are They When You Need Them?

"Where are the pied pipers of promiscuity when you need them?" people are beginning to wonder. Who are these sultans of sex and gurus of sleaze who sell us the movies, television shows, magazines, and products that titillate and seduce us but leave us empty? Why have we listened to men and women whose consciences are governed only by their bank accounts? Where is Planned Parenthood when a sixteen-year-old girl they convinced to get an abortion (without telling her parents) commits suicide because she couldn't handle the guilt? Where is the judicial system and parole board when your eight-year-old son is forced into sodomy by a repeat offender they let out of prison? Where is the ACLU when your sister is tortured and raped by a pornography addict glutted with the sado-masochistic mind-poison they've defended with the First Amendment? Where are the gender-diluting feminists and gay activists when your family is ripped apart by the pain of one member's submersion into the homosexual subculture? Where are the romance novelists when a girl has given herself sexually only to men she's loved, but all of them are gone, and she is left lonely and bitter? Where is the television scriptwriter, magazine editor, or novelist when your wife is finally convinced the grass is greener elsewhere and leaves you for another man?

While the media glorify affairs, many find out the hard way they've been lied to. In a recent survey of women, 40 percent indicated they had extramarital affairs, three-fourths of those because they were emotionally unsatisfied with their husbands. However, less than half the women who had affairs said they even enjoyed extramarital sex—not to mention the devastating consequences.[6]

Some women are waking up to the infuriating truth: rather than benefiting from it (as they've been incessantly told), they are, in fact, the revolution's victims. Though the sexual revolution told women their sexual nature was like men's—that they could enjoy sex without commitment—millions have found out the hard way that this is simply a lie.

Why Women Are the Revolution's Greatest Victims

The issue of gender differences is aptly addressed by anthropologist Donald Symons in *The Evolution of Human Sexuality*. He believes the acid test of the extent of male-female sexual differences is found in homosexual relationships—where men and women are not forced to compromise with the opposite sex.

There is a substantial male homosexual market for pornography and no lesbian market whatsoever. This suggests that the tendency to be sexually aroused by "objectified" visual stimuli is simply a male tendency, not an expression of contempt for women.

The tremendous importance of physical attractiveness and youth in determining sexual desirability among both homosexual and heterosexual men implies that these criteria are relatively innate in men.

Knowledge of a potential partner's character—even via a brief conversation—can sometimes diminish a male's sexual interest by interfering with his fantasies. A female's sexual interest usually requires knowledge of the partner's character and prior involvement. Among men, sex sometimes results in intimacy; among women, intimacy sometimes results in sex.

The tendency to desire and enjoy sexual variety appears to be a male proclivity, manifested by homosexual men to an unprecedented degree only because their behavior is not constrained by the necessity of compromising with women.

That homosexual men behave in many ways like heterosexual men, only more so, and lesbians behave in many ways like heterosexual women, only more so, indicates that some aspects of human sexuality are not so plastic after all.[6]

The sexual revolution's bread and butter has been the fallacy that women can enjoy promiscuity as readily as men—that gender equality in fact *demands* that they do so. A *NBC Reports* interviewed many women sucked into the promiscuity but now tired of sex games. They admit now they haven't enjoyed their liberated lives. What they really want is to be married and have a family.

C. S. Lewis, in the last piece he wrote for publication, said:

A society in which conjugal infidelity is tolerated must always be in the long run a society adverse to women. Women, whatever a few male songs and satires may say to the contrary, are more naturally monogamous than men; it is a biological necessity. Where promiscuity prevails, they will therefore always be more often the victims than the culprits.[7]

Traditionally, men married women, among other reasons, because commitment was the horse that pulled the cart of sexual intimacy. But the sexual revolution put the cart before the horse. Not only women, but all of society now suffers, for man is at his best when made faithful and responsible in a marriage and family setting.

Promiscuity rips at the seams of a civilized society. It has been tried and found wanting, but countless millions suffer because it has been tried and millions more continue to try it and make their discoveries the hard way. The reader who hasn't yet gone the route of sexual experimentation could save himself and his family a lot of grief by learning the lesson from others. Sexual immorality is a dead end street. Fortunately, some are beginning to realize this, and marital fidelity is winning back some lost ground.

Diseases of Promiscuity—Nature Strikes Back

Sexually transmitted diseases (STDs), are one of God-created nature's ways of reminding us that we aren't built to be promiscuous. Gonorrhea is still at epidemic proportions, and some of its strains are increasingly resistant to antibiotics. Syphilis still rears its ugly head, as do venereal warts and about twenty other lesser known diseases of promiscuity.

Called "the new scarlet letter," herpes had a profound effect on sexual behavior:

> Among its more subliminal effects, herpes has returned to sex its former shadings of corruption and sin. The virus has come to symbolize massive guilt; it's viewed as the mark of an angry God punishing people for the sins of the sexual revolution. The irony is that it's just those who pioneered the revolution who are most likely afflicted with the disease. . . .[8]

A thirty-six-year-old bachelor, fearful of the disease stated, "Herpes did for me what no therapist was ever able to do . . . it forces me to get to know someone before I go to bed with her.[9]

Shortly after the first wave of the herpes epidemic came, the terrifying disease AIDS emerged in the homosexual community. Spread beyond homosexuals, the fear of AIDS has become a deterent to casual sex, forcing people to ask themselves questions God gave the answers to long ago.

A Return to Biblical Morality?

Unquestionably, the advent of herpes and AIDS and other diseases has spawned an ad hoc sexual conservativism.

The dread of disease, however, is a far cry from the only true and lasting moral reform, one based on firm moral foundations.

We should be grateful for any swing away from promiscuity but not necessarily impressed by it—any more than we would be impressed with the moral reform of a burglar who curtails his unethical behavior for fear of burglar alarms and homeowners with guns. AIDS and STDs have brought temporary fear, not lasting repentance and transformation. Once a cure for these and other diseases is effected, the door to "safe" promiscuity will open again, and those whose moral reformation is based merely on self-preservation will be the first to barge through.

Is the Sexual Revolution Over?

Time magazine's cover declared: "Sex in the '80s: The Revolution Is Over." *Is* the revolution really over? In one sense, yes, it is over. If that's the good news, though, here's the bad—the wrong side won.

No revolution is over until someone has won. If the sexual revolution was against the traditional Judeo-Christian morality based on Scripture, and that revolution is over, then biblical morality lost.

What we are witnessing—a new freedom in discussing sex, and promoting it, and experimenting with it—is not the Sexual Revolution, but the followup action that implements the Revolution. The Revolution is over in the sense that there is now no possibility that we shall return to the state of affairs that existed in the past. From now on, we shall slowly adjust our attitudes and behavior to the new concept which seems certain in time to gain almost universal acceptance.[10]

Sexual morality without biblical absolutes is a house without a foundation, a ship destined to sink. Sexual reform without a return to the authority of Scripture is ultimately as fruitless as rearranging the furniture on the *Titanic* (though it might improve the quality of life on the *Titanic* in the meantime).

The real question is not "Has the sexual revolution left us?" but "*Where* has it left us?"

The new conservativism is no victory for puritans. No sexual counter-revolution is underway. The sexual revolution has not been rebuffed, merely absorbed into the culture.[11]

Apart from a widespread national return to God, never again will the followers of Christ be able to take their sexual cues from this society. We must be counter-revolutionaries, fending for ourselves, forging out our own biblical ethic, and implementing it in our personal lives, families and churches. In the process we must open wide our doors and invite in those weary pilgrims made open to the Christian faith because they have tasted the bitter waters of the world's sorry alternative.

Chapter 6, Notes

1. George Leonard, "The End of Sex," *Esquire*, December 1982, 74.

2. Rollo May, *Love and Will* (New York: W. W. Norton and Co., 1969), 63.

3. Leonard, "End of Sex," 74, 78.

4. Fran Schumer, "Is Sex Dead?" *New York*, 6 December 1982, 69.

5. John Leo, "The Revolution Is Over," *Time*, 9 April 1984, 75.

6. *USA Today*, 19 April 1983, sec. D.

7. *USA Today*, 5 July 1983, sec. D.

8. Donald Symons, "He Versus She," *Science Digest*, December 1983, 86.

9. C. S. Lewis, "We Have No 'Right to Happiness'," *God in the Dock* (Grand Rapids, Mich.: Wm. B. Eerdmans Publishing Co., 1970), 321.

10. Schumer, "Is Sex Dead?" 91.

11. Ibid., 88.

12. David Mace, *The Christian Response to the Sexual Revolution*, (Nashville: Abingdon Press, 1970), 68.

13. John Leo, "The Revolution is over," *Time*, 9 April 1984, 83.

PART 3

God Has Something to Say

CHAPTER 7

Sex: God's Gift to Humanity

In a cover story in the science magazine *Discover*, the question was asked, "Why sex?"

> Sex is an inefficient, risky way for an organism to reproduce itself. . . . Sex, the scientists say, requires an inordinate amount of time and energy. . . . Because sex diminishes a parent's genetic tie to its offspring, it contradicts a basic biological tenet: that the main goal of an organism is to transmit as many of its genes as possible to the next generation. In fact, sex dictates that a parent can pass on only half its genes to each of its progeny.
>
> Asexual reproduction (without sex) seems a likelier

choice for nature to make. It is faster and more efficient, and it allows a creature both to replicate itself without the bother of mating, and to procure offspring that carry all of its genes. If by some fluke sex happens to arise in a species, theoretically it should not take hold; the sexual creatures should soon be supplanted by the original asexual stock.

Says George Williams, a population biologist of the State University of New York at Stony Brook, "At first glance, and second, and third, it appears that sex shouldn't have evolved." Indeed, the persistence of sex is one of the fundamental mysteries in evolutionary biology today.[1]

After further exploring what they call "the paradox of sex" and "the riddle of sex," the authors come to this fascinating conclusion:

> Are biologists any closer to an answer than they were fifty years ago? Perhaps not. Says John Maynard Smith of the University of Sussex, in England, one of the leading students of the mystery, "One is left with the feeling that some essential feature of the situation is being overlooked."[2]

The scientist's feeling is justified. There *is* an essential feature of the situation being overlooked. His colleague was right also—sex shouldn't have evolved. In fact, it didn't. It was created by the greatest "overlooked essential feature" in the universe.

In the Beginning Was Sex

God is the architect, engineer, and builder of sex. It *is* a carefully planned facet of our humanity, created for our good and

His glory. Anyone who questions whether sex is good, questions whether God is good. The rightness and legitimacy of sex stand or fall with the morally pure character of the One who created it.

To put sex in perspective, we must begin at the beginning—creation. Having fashioned man and woman with their distinctive sexual natures, "God blessed them and said to them, 'Be fruitful and increase in number; fill the earth and subdue it'" (Genesis 1:28).

The divine command to reproduce required the sexual merger of man and woman. This was one command they were happy to obey (unlike our scientists, they did not consider mating a bother). Sex was part and parcel of Eden's paradise.

God confers His stamp of approval on each facet of his creation. All that He had made was devoid of blemish or flaw; all of creation was declared good (Genesis 1: 10, 12, 18, 25). Yet, following the creation of man, God says there is something "not good" (Genesis 2:18). What was not good was that Adam was alone.

But Adam was not just lonely—God's solution was not to create other men for companionship. Only a woman could fill the void. Following the creation of Eve, "God saw all that he had made, and it was very good." What was included in that which was very good? Maleness. Femaleness. Sexuality. Sex.

"It was good," "it was good," "it was good," "it was good," "it was not good," "it was very good." Creation was incomplete until the debut of the second sex. God never intended a unisex humanity.

Eve was like Adam, yet unlike him. Same humanity, different gender. Man and woman were equal but not the same.

Their oneness was not a uniformity stemming from sameness, but a unity transcending differentness.

This marvelous integration was culminated in their sexual union: "For this reason a man will leave his father and mother and be united to his wife, and they will become one flesh" (Genesis 2:24). Man and woman consummate marriage through God-ordained sexual union. This means not just the blending of bodies, but also the merging of minds, the assimilating of souls.

Genesis 2, the last account of a world without sin, ends gloriously with two sexual beings, unclothed and unashamed, free to enjoy sex. God looks on their nakedness and their sexual union with the smile of complete approval.

Sex Is Someone You Are

God designed the sexual union to be a truly intimate experience. This is demonstrated by the primary word for sexual intercourse used in the Old Testament, the Hebrew word *yadah*, "to know." "Now Adam knew Eve his wife, and she conceived and bore Cain" (Genesis 4: 1, RSV).

Yadah speaks of an intimacy wherein two parties see each other as they truly are. The concept is not of some distant objective, or academic acquaintance but a personal, intimate, and experiential knowledge of another. *Yadah* is the same word that is used of a believer's relationship with his God (e.g. Daniel 11:32). To know one's marriage partner in the act of sex is analogous to developing intimacy with God.

Our word *intercourse* suggests this. Sexual intercourse is an interpersonal *communicative* experience with one to whom we are exclusively and unconditionally committed. There is nothing even remotely casual or impersonal about sex.

Many, perhaps most, pagan religions incorporated sexual relations into their worship of false deities because of the metaphysical dimension of the sex act. Somehow, sexual intercourse was thought to forge a link between the pagan worshipers and the personages that inhabited the spiritual world. A Chinese proverb says, "Sexual intercourse is the human counterpart of the cosmic process."

Writers have compared sex to the opening of a door and a peek into Heaven, where the soul temporarily leaves the body. Certainly the Christian worshiper who enjoys the God-intended role of sex in his marriage can regard his experience as a spiritual one. Regardless of our denominational backgrounds, should we not see something sacramental about marriage? And if marriage, also sex, the bond of marriage. In its rightful place, sexual expression transcends the boundaries of the physical and propels its participants into the realm of the spiritual.

We must distinguish between sexuality and sexual activity. My sexuality exists independently of what I do. It is a matter of identity, not behavior. God is the author of all sexuality and the personal creator of my sexuality. Sexuality exists independently of marriage or the sex act. Jesus was a sexual being, though he did not marry or engage in sex. To be human is to be sexual. The two are inseparably linked. Sex is not just something you do. Sex is someone you are.

George Gilder points out our loss in reducing sex to a physical act:

> The words no longer evoke an image of a broad pageant of relations and differences between the sexes, embracing every aspect of our lives. Instead "sex" and "sexuality" are assumed to refer chiefly to copulation, as if our sexual lives

were restricted to the male limits—as if the experiences of maternity were not paramount sexual events. In fact, however, our whole lives are sexual. Sexual energy animates most of our activities and connects every individual to a family and a community. Sexuality is best examined not in terms of sexology, physiology, or psychology, but as a study encompassing all the ulterior life of our society.[3]

Sexuality is not confined to the sex drive, though it certainly embraces it. Freud was wrong about many of his sexual notions, but right when he insisted that the sex drive is a powerful force that affects the entire personality. Channeled properly, it is a boon to human creativity and the advancement of culture.

As an extension of our sexuality, sexual thoughts and actions are more than just something we think or do. They are something we are, and someone we are becoming. Having sex with someone is so much more than sharing a bed. It is sharing a life, surrendering one's inner self to another. Within God's intended context it is beautiful. Outside, it is not.

No matter how flippantly we treat sex, it will never be flippant with us. There is nothing casual about sex, nothing simple or isolated about the act of sex. A direct link exists between sex and the human soul. Whenever a person has sex, he lays his life on the line.

The Reason for Sex

Since early Church history there have been those who believe the only purpose for sex is to prevent the cessation of humanity (no sex, no people). These people assume, I suppose, that a Christian couple with four children has had sexual intercourse twice as often as a couple with two. It is this kind of antisexual attitude that drove society to sexual repression and set the stage for the sexual revolution.

The argument that sex is only for procreation is as unimaginative as it is old. Couldn't an all-knowing Creator devise some other means considerably more simple, dependable, and refined that would serve the solitary purpose of procreation? If He wanted to, He could have married couples set out a crib on the back porch whenever they wanted another child (sort of a tooth fairy approach to family planning). But to the delight of some and the chagrin of others, God has made procreation only one function of that multi-dimensional experience called sex.

Of course, procreation is a major purpose of sex and the birth control revolution has served to bury and discredit that reality. But when we consider that even without contraceptives the vast majority of times a couple has sex will not result in conception, we must realize there is much more to sex than procreation.

We should not feel compelled to choose between sex as a means of procreation and sex as a means of pleasure, as if the two are mutually exclusive. Both are intended by God, as is the expression and cultivation of spiritual and emotional oneness in marriage. To reduce sex to nothing more than a means to the end of childbearing is to miss the point of the marital oneness implicit in the one-flesh relationship.

The body is to be an instrument of the spirit, and the uniting of bodies is in its essence the uniting of spirits (1 Corinthians 6:15-17). Note that the immediate context of Genesis 2:24, where the sexual union is first specifically mentioned, says nothing about bearing children. In that passage the exclusive concern is the present act of marriage, not the future potential of parenting.

As surely as God is the creator of sex and sex drives, He is the designer of the physical and psychological pleasures woven into sex. It was not Satan who made sex pleasurable to push us toward sin, but God who made it pleasurable to pull us toward fulfillment.

If you doubt this, consider the fact that one part of the female anatomy, the clitoris, serves no other function than to give women a sensation of pleasure in sex. Obviously, God made sex to be enjoyed.

Solomon on Sex

If the Genesis account and the created nature of sex are not enough to convince us that it is a pure and beautiful gift from God, the clear statements of Proverbs and the Song of Solomon should end all debate. Note the poetic expressions of sexual intimacy and fidelity in the following passage from Proverbs:

> Drink water from your own cistern,
>   running water from your own well.
> Should your springs overflow in the streets,
>   your streams of water in the public squares?
> Let them be yours alone,
>   never to be shared with strangers.
> May your fountain be blessed,
>   and may you rejoice in the wife of your youth.
> A loving doe, a graceful deer—
>   may her breasts satisfy you always,
>   may you ever be captivated by her love.
> Why be captivated, my son, by an adulteress?
>   Why embrace the bosom of another man's wife?
>
> (Proverbs 5:15-20)

God wants sex to be enjoyed so much in marriage that there will be no compulsion to have sex outside of marriage. This passage, as well as others, demonstrates that a positive (yes, erotic) sex life in a marriage is one of the greatest guards against sexual impurity. Note that Solomon does not deal only with intercourse but with love play ("May her breasts satisfy you always"), showing again that pleasure is a legitimate part of sex, even pleasure that has no direct reproductive purpose.

Should Proverbs' message of sexual pleasure in marriage fall on deaf ears, the Song of Solomon thunders the same message at a decibel level too high to ignore. The Song of Solomon takes us into a beautiful dialogue between two newlyweds. Young Solomon's message to Shulamith, his bride, includes such erotic exclamations as these:

> Your breasts are like two fawns,
>> like twin fawns of a gazelle
>> that browse among the lilies (4:5).

> How delightful is your love, my sister, my bride!
>> How much more pleasing is your love than wine,
>> and the fragrance of your perfume than any spice! (4:10).

> Your graceful legs are like jewels,
>> the work of a craftsman's hands.
> How beautiful you are and how pleasing,
>> O love, with your delights!
> Your stature is like that of the palm,
>> and your breasts like clusters of fruit.
> I said, "I will climb the palm tree;
>> I will take hold of its fruit."
> May your breasts be like the clusters of the vine,

the fragrance of your breath like apples,
and your mouth like the best wine (7:1, 6-9).

Even to the English reader, the sexual tone of these expressions is unmistakable. But to the Hebrew, who readily understood many of the poetic metaphors lost on us, the Song was throughout an unashamedly erotic expression of marital love.

In 7:1-9 the husband describes his wife's naked body in great detail. Rather than being ashamed or embarrassed by this, she is pleased and responds, "I belong to my lover, and his desire is for me" (7: 10). In the following verses she invites him to come away and spend the night, then go early in the morning to the vineyard, and promises, "there I will give you my love" (vv. 11-12). Obviously, this God-fearing wife is just as interested in sex as her husband.

For too long the Song of Solomon has been avoided, ignored, or allegorized into oblivion. The fact that God chose to include it in His Word should tell us something about the sanctity of sex.

Jesus and Paul on Sex

The New Testament consistently maintains the same exalted view of sexual union in marriage that is established in the Old. Jesus endorsed married love not only implicitly by his attendance and assistance at the wedding at Cana (John 2) but explicitly in Matthew 19:4-6:

"Haven't you read," he replied, "that at the beginning the Creator 'made them male and female,' and said, 'For this reason a man will leave his father and mother and be united to his wife, and the two will become one flesh'? So they are no longer two, but one. Therefore what God has joined together, let man not separate."

In Ephesians 5:25-33 the apostle Paul makes a direct comparison between a husband's love for his wife and Christ's love for his bride, the Church. Christ is the model of personal sacrificial giving of self for the highest good of the beloved. In verses 31-32 Paul illustrates the intimate union of Christ and his bride with the marital sexual union of man and wife. What a tribute to marriage and marital sex to be chosen for such a comparison!

It's also interesting that Christ gives Himself for His bride in a way that makes her "holy," "radiant," "without stain and blameless" (vv. 25-27). Husbands are commanded to do the very same for their wives (v. 28). The husband is responsible to cultivate and maintain his wife's purity sexually and in every way. To enjoy a sexual relationship with her is to express his love and further engender hers.

In 1 Corinthians, Paul affirms sexual intercourse as basic to maintaining the sexual purity of a marriage. Sexual intercourse is not just conceded, permitted, or expected in a marriage. It is explicitly *commanded*:

> The husband should fulfill his marital duty to his wife, and likewise the wife to her husband. The wife's body does not belong to her alone but also to her husband. In the same way, the husband's body does not belong to him alone but also to his wife. Do not deprive each other except by mutual consent and for a time, so that you may devote yourselves to prayer. Then come together again so that Satan will not

tempt you because of your lack of self control (1 Corinthians 7:3-5).

Many couples are glad to obey, but for others this is a major problem. We must realize that carnality surfaces not only in sexual promiscuity but in the selfishness that sexually denies one's marriage partner. It is not enough for us to say that sex is a marital privilege. It *is* that, but it is also a sacred responsibility. When carried out consistently, it serves to protect the moral fiber of the marriage relationship.

Resisting the Antibodies

If Scripture is so clear on the matter, why have Christians tended to be so negative toward sex? The problem began early in Church history, when theology was strongly influenced by Greek philosophy.

The Hebrews were holistic in their perceptions of life. God made the body, God made sex, God made marriage, of which sex was a part. Marriage was good, sex was good. Very simple—and very accurate.

Greek thought, on the contrary, was characterized by a dualism in which the spiritual world was good, and the physical world was bad. Plato, for example, called the body a "prison" that held captive the soul.

In the early centuries A.D. there were two schools of Greek thought: Stoicism and Epicureanism. The Stoics treated their bodies harshly, denying themselves even the most simple pleasures. Spirituality, to them, consisted of depriving themselves of all comfort and pleasure. In contrast, the Epicureans readily indulged their bodies, gratifying every appetite. While very different in behavior, the Stoics and Epicureans shared a common disregard for the body. The Stoics demeaned it, so refused to satisfy it. The Epicureans demeaned it, so felt free to abuse it in the pursuit of pleasure.

Early Christians, who tended toward legalism, adopted Stoic philosophy and lifestyles. Believers elevating personal liberty gravitated toward Epicurean ideals and behavior. Christians on both extremes tended to view the body as vulgar and base.

C. S. Lewis spoke of Christians to whom the body was "'a sack of dung,' food for worms, filthy, shameful, a source of nothing but temptation to bad men and humiliation to good ones."[4] Origen carried this philosophy to the extreme by castrating himself in a vain attempt to solve the problem of lust.

Sometimes the apostle Paul is accused, even by Christians, of fostering this tragic disdain for the human body. The notion that Paul's view was "sex is of the flesh" betrays a common but serious misunderstanding of Pauline theology.[6] Certainly, Paul maintained consistently that sexual *immorality* is of the flesh. But what is the flesh? In Paul's writings, the flesh is not synonymous with the body. Rather, the flesh is the sin principle, the depraved force that influences a man toward sin, prompting him to misuse the members of his body to disobey God. While Paul speaks of the flesh as the Christian's enemy, he speaks of the body as the temple of the Holy Spirit (1 Corinthians 6:19). If the shekinah glory of God dwells within our bodies, surely they are not inherently sinful!

When the Christians of Corinth were indulging in the excesses of gluttony and immorality, Paul reminded them their bodies were "for the Lord, and the Lord for the body" (1 Corinthians 6:13). Furthermore, the bodies they were abusing would be raised up and inhabited for all eternity (6:14). Indeed, Paul devotes all of chapter 15 of the same book to the resurrection of the body, a concept held in disdain by the Greeks, who wanted only to rid themselves of their bodily prison.

Paul sees consecration as the submitting of the body to do the will of God (Romans 12:1-2). He is careful to discipline his body (1 Corinthians 9:27), but never to degrade it. He says the body is the temple of the Holy Spirit, and that the Christian can glorify God with his body (1 Corinthians 6:19-20). He even compares the holy Church of God to a human body, with Christ represented by the head (1 Corinthians 12:14-27). Properly understood, Paul was not anti-body!

"Your hands made me and formed me," the psalmist says to his Lord (119:73). David expressed to God, "You knit me together in my mother's womb. I praise you because I am fearfully and wonderfully made" (Psalm 139:13-14). The body, including its sex organs and sex drives, is something to thank God for, not be ashamed of.

Christ's incarnation is permanent proof that the body is not sinful. The human body is compatible with deity—God was not too good to inhabit a body! Jesus' body never made him sinful. Heaven will be inhabited by redeemed bodies, both Christ's and ours.

If our bodies are good and sex is not sinful, why must we cover our bodies from each other? Because human hearts are sinful. Clothes lessen the visual stimuli that prompt fallen beings to treat others as sex objects and to lust after sex outside its God-intended context. Within marriage, God's ideal is still that of paradise where there was no shame in beholding each other's nakedness (Genesis 2:25).

A New Perspective

There you have it. The body was not put together by a pervert. Sex was not invented in a dark alley behind a porno shop. It was made in Heaven—where purity reigns. As Christians, we must look at sex through the eyes of God.

The Church needs to scrape off the barnacles of unbiblical tradition and unscientific superstition so that a wholesome view of sex can appear. We cannot afford any longer the excess baggage of negativism. The harm that this heresy has done is immeasurable because it has robbed men and women of the ability to appreciate and enjoy sex as God intended.[7]

Despite the bad press given it by misguided believers, sex is God's gift to humanity. In marriage, let us celebrate sex. May husband and wife never be ashamed to enjoy together what God was not ashamed to create.

Chapter 8, Notes

1. Gina Maranto and Shannon Brownlee, "Why Sex?" *Discover*, February 1984, 24.

2. Ibid., 28.

3. George Gilder, *Sexual Suicide* (New York: New York Times Book Co., 1973), 1-2.

4. Joseph C. Dillow, *Solomon on Sex* (Nashville: Thomas Nelson Publishers, 1977).

5. C. S. Lewis, *The Four Loves* (New York: Harcourt Brace Jovanovich, 1960),142-43.

6. Ray E. Short, *Sex, Love or Infatuation* (Minneapolis: Augsburg Publishing House, 1978), 93.

7. Harry Hollis, "A Christian Model for Sexual Understanding and Behavior," in *Secrets of Our Sexuality*, ed. Gary Collins, (Waco, Tex.: Word Books, 1976), 82.

CHAPTER 8

When Sex Becomes Sin

"How can anything so good be so bad?" If sex is as good as we portrayed it in the previous chapter, why is it that many sexual acts are condemned in Scripture? The answer is that like most good things, sex was created to exist within prescribed boundaries. As long as it stays within those boundaries, it is good. The moment it moves outside them, it becomes bad.

Take water and fire as examples. Water is a great gift of God. Without it we would die. Yet when water is out of control, when it violates its proper boundaries, it can wreak terrible destruction—as anyone knows who has seen a flood or a tidal wave. Fire is likewise a great gift of God, but when out of control it can destroy a house, decimate a forest, and inflict painful and horrible death.

The best gifts of God are powerful, and when out of control that power becomes ruinous. So it is with sex. Sex outside marriage is so bad precisely because sex inside marriage is so good.

God's Will Is Not Lost

Many of us spend great energy, time, and money trying to "find God's will" (with the implication that it's somehow lost or obscure). But there's no mystery about God's will in most matters of sexual behavior:

> It is God's will that you should be holy; that you should avoid sexual immorality; that each of you should learn to control his own body in a way that is holy and honorable, not in passionate lust like the heathen, who do not know God; and that in this matter no one should wrong his brother or take advantage of him. The Lord will punish men for all such sins, as we have already told you and warned you. For God did not call us to be impure, but to live a holy life. Therefore, he who rejects this instruction does not reject man but God, who gives you his Holy Spirit (1 Thessalonians 4:3-8).

The apostle Paul considers our personal holiness inseparable from our sexual behavior. There is no holiness where there is immorality. Like oil and water, the two do not mix. If we violate God's sexual standards, no matter what else we do or don't do, we simply cannot be in God's will. We need to pray for power to accomplish His will in sexual matters but not to find out what that will is. Scripture makes it clear.

The Moral Climate of Biblical Times

The biblical standards of sexual morality stood in stark contrast to the accepted social norms of most of the ancient cultures. The people of Israel were surrounded by heathen nations characterized not only by pagan worship but the grossest forms of immorality. Canaanite religions featured the worship of phallic fertility gods and multi-breasted goddesses, and their rituals often included lewd dances followed by sexual intercourse and full-scale orgies. Prostitutes, both male and female, were a central part of the temple worship.

While the societies in the New Testament era were generally more civilized than the Canaanites, their sexual mores were just as bad. The Greek writings of Plato, Lucian, and many others elevated homosexuality. Immorality was a way of life in Greek cities like ancient Corinth, where a thousand prostitutes, priestesses of Aphrodite, walked the streets and gave their fees to the temple priests. In time, the city's name was coined in a verb form (*corinthiazomai*) that actually meant to have intercourse with a prostitute.

The Christians in New Testament Corinth lived in a new city built a hundred years after ancient Corinth was destroyed. Nevertheless, the same spirit of immorality prevailed, still rooted in the mingling of pagan religion and immorality (2 Corinthians 6:15-20). No wonder the Corinthian Christians, raised in this environment had such struggles with sexual temptation.

Taking their cue from the rampant immorality of the Greek culture they assimilated, Roman emperors set a national example of notorious immorality. The emperor Caligula lived in incest with his sister, as did Nero with his own mother. Nero also married a young man. Julius Caesar was likewise a known homosexual, and the emperor Hadrian was extremely promiscuous with men and women alike.

Promiscuity was the norm, fidelity was a foreign concept. But the fledgling Christian faith did not surrender to the secular drift, insisting that those who named the name of Christ live in sexual purity: "Chastity was the one completely new virtue which Christianity introduced into the pagan world."[1] It was a distinction so basic, so fundamental, that the absence of purity would nullify the credibility of the Gospel. No wonder it is repeatedly stressed in the New Testament epistles.

> But among you there must not be even a hint of sexual immorality, or of any kind of impurity, or of greed, because these are improper for God's holy people. Nor should there be obscenity, foolish talk or coarse joking, which are out of place, but rather thanksgiving. For of this you can be sure: No immoral, impure or greedy person—such a man is an idolater—has any inheritance in the kingdom of Christ and of God. Let no one deceive you with empty words, for because of such things God's wrath comes on those who are disobedient. Therefore do not be partners with them (Ephesians 5:3-7).

Other passages specifically state that those living in sexual immorality will not inherit the kingdom of God (I Corinthians 6:9-10; Revelation 22:14-15). These verses are hard to reconcile with the grim reality of sexual sin among Christians. Even if we do not know what to make of them, however, they demonstrate how much God hates sexual sin. They also show the basic incompatibility of the new life in Christ and the life of immorality. Simply put, Scripture leaves no place for sexual impurity in the Christian life, Christian family, or Christian Church.

A Closer Look at Scripture's View of Immorality

Scripture uses many terms for sexual immorality. Some of these are close synonyms, and many have overlapping meanings. To summarize, under Old Testament law there were four readily identifiable major categories of sexual sin:

1. *Fornication*: any sexual relations outside of marriage, including those between two unmarried people.
2. *Adultery*: sexual relations with someone other than one's spouse or with the spouse of another.
3. *Homosexuality*: sexual relations between two people of the same gender—males with males or females with females.
4. *Bestiality*: sexual relations with an animal.

Other sexual crimes are specifically addressed but fall under one or more of these categories. Rape and incest, for instance, are particularly despicable brands of fornication that might also be adultery or homosexuality, depending on who is involved.

Still other sexual sins are dealt with not in precept, but in principle. When Ham looked upon the nakedness of his father Noah and told his brothers, they walked into Noah's tent backwards to cover him, being careful not to look (Genesis 9:20-27). While commentators disagree on precisely what Ham was guilty of, Noah's severe reaction makes clear that his actions or attitude were highly inappropriate. Presumably, choosing to look at and tell others of his father's nakedness demonstrated a disrespect for his sexual sanctity and privacy. This principle has application both to those who display their nudity to others and those who delight in gazing at the nudity of others.

LUST: THE BATTLE IN YOUR MIND

The sex drive is powerful. Many say it is just another urge, like hunger and thirst, and sexual intercourse just another biological function. Animals eat, drink, sleep, excrete, and copulate, and people are animals, so . . .

But Paul tells the Corinthians something different:

> Food was meant for the stomach and the stomach for food; but God has no permanent purpose for either. But you cannot say that our physical body was made for sexual promiscuity; it was made for the Lord, and in the Lord is the answer to its needs (1 Corinthians 6:13, Phillips).

Paul insists that the analogy between satisfying our hunger for food and indulging our sexual desires is invalid. "Natural" does not always mean "right." While other urges exist for our physical maintenance, sex does not. We will die without food and water. We will not die without sex. Sex is never an emergency, immorality never a necessity. Lust, however, tells us otherwise.

What Does Scripture Say About Lust?

Sexual lust is condemned in the Old Testament. As we briefly noted in the previous chapter, the Tenth Commandment prohibits the coveting of another person's marriage partner (Exodus 20:17). In vivid detail Proverbs repeatedly warns against the lust toward immorality, saying it is the fool who gives in to lust and the wise who resists it (Proverbs 2:16-19; 5:1-23; 6:23-29).

We can learn a great deal about lust through the examples,

primarily negative, of Samson and Delilah, David and Bathsheba, and Hosea and Gomer. The prophets' picture of Israel as God's unfaithful wife also portrays the ugliness of lust and immorality (Jeremiah 3, Ezekiel 16). But the key to the entire biblical teaching on lust is found in Jesus' Sermon on the Mount:

> "You have heard that it was said, 'Do not commit adultery.' But I tell you that anyone who looks at a woman lustfully has already committed adultery with her in his heart" (Matthew 5:27-28).

Jesus cuts to the moral root of the command. He recognizes that morality resides first in the heart or the mind. Pharisees emphasized the eternal, as if one could live up to God's standards just by refraining from a physical act. Jesus raised the moral bar, saying that lust is not only the source of sexual sin, but is itself sin. He closed the door to the notion of the Pharisees that a man could undress a woman in his mind and remain pure. Lust is not the initial temptation toward sin, but is mentally succumbing to that temptation. We are to call upon our resources in Christ and be transformed by the renewing of our minds (Romans 12:2). We are to deny and put to death lust when it tries to get a grip on us (Colossians 3:5). We're to fill our minds with what is pure (Philippians 4:8).

Lust is the counterfeit of love. Satan wants nothing more than that we should fail to see the difference between the two. At its root, lust is absolutely selfish; it uses another to gratify itself. Love, on the contrary, always acts in the best interests of the other person. "Love can always wait to give—lust can never wait to get."

Sexual Sin Is Never "Out of the Blue"

Doug was a seminary student preparing for the ministry. One night he had an argument with his wife. Upset, he left home, drove to a nearby restaurant and tried to think things through over a cup of coffee. Soon Doug was engrossed in conversation with a young woman in the next booth. A few hours later, he was in bed with her.

Doug came to me ashamed and distressed. "How can I tell my wife? Will she ever forgive me?" he asked. "It was so sudden—there was no warning. *Why did God let this happen?*"

Mike is a successful executive, church leader, and family man. One day he met an attractive woman in an elevator and thought she was flirting with him. Before he knew it, Mike asked her to come into his office and undress in front of him. Fortunately, she refused. But Mike was shocked at what he had done (and might have done had she complied). "What is happening to me?" he asked. "How could I do something like this?"

From appearances, it seemed that Doug and Mike fell into sexual sin suddenly, without warning. But that was not the case.

Doug had worked nonstop to put himself through seminary. He came to subtly resent Joan, his wife, seeing her and the children as obstacles to his goal of graduating and entering the ministry. It had been two years since he had spent any meaningful time alone with Joan or communicated on other than a superficial level. Their relationship was stale, but both lacked the time or energy to change it.

When Joan and the children were visiting relatives, Doug took an evening break from his theology paper to get some fresh air. He ended up at an X-rated movie. Afterwards, every time he had sex with Joan he pretended she was a woman from the movie. He felt guilty, yet it didn't appear to do any real harm.

What happened to Mike actually began years before he asked that girl to undress in his office. He had a problem with lust. Far worse, he failed to recognize or deal with that problem. On his lunch hour Mike often stopped by a convenience store to buy a paper or pack of gum. Invariably he wandered to the magazine rack and paged through *Hustler* or *Penthouse*. He never intended to (so he told himself). But he always did.

The same mind that wanted to serve Christ permitted itself to indulge in lustful fantasies. One day Mike's mind, programmed by the immoral images he had fed it, prompted him to immoral action.

Sexual sin never comes out of the blue. It is the predictable result of a long natural process in which a mind susceptible to sin is granted unguarded exposure to immoral input.

It's All in Your Mind

"Sow a thought, reap an action; sow an action, reap a habit; sow a habit, reap a character; sow a character, reap a destiny."

We are what we think. Today's thoughts are the stuff of which tomorrow's character is made. Temptation may come suddenly, but sin does not. Neither does moral and spiritual fiber. It is the result of a process—a process over which we *do* have control. The best way to guard against tomorrow's sexual temptations is to cultivate a pure mind today, a mind saturated not in the world's input but in God's.

Our sexual morality is the sum of a continuous series of

choices, decisions, and actions, including all those tiny indulgences and minuscule compromises. Like a photographic
plate accumulating light to form an image, our mind is the
cumulative result of all we expose it to—whether godly or
ungodly.

Male or female, young or old, Christian or non-Christian,
all of us face a battle for sexual purity. The enemy is lust, the
stakes are high, the reward is the peace and pleasure of purity.

And the battle is in our minds.

Chapter 8, Notes

1. William Barclay, *Flesh and Spirit* (Grand Rapids, Mich.: Baker Book House, 1976), 27.

CHAPTER 9

The Consequences of Sexual Sin

"**W**hy shouldn't single people get in on sex?" The question came from the audience of a popular television talk show and was directed at the panel of three Christian authors and their wives.

"We're not saying that unmarried people can't get a kick out of sex," came the reply. "We're just saying we believe in God's commandments. They're written on stone, and you can't break them without them breaking you!"

The Law of the Harvest

Violating God's sexual standards is like violating the law of gravity—it has a way of catching up with you. The laws apply regardless of who believes in them and who doesn't. The unbeliever lives in the same moral universe—*God's universe*—as the believer and is therefore liable to the same moral laws (one need not believe in the law of gravity to be subject to it).

> Do not be deceived: God cannot be mocked. A man reaps what he sows. The one who sows to please his sinful nature, from that nature will reap destruction; the one who sows to please the Spirit, from the Spirit will reap eternal life (Galatians 6:7-8).

The Christian who treats sex with sanctity, elevating it in marriage and rejecting it outside, will be blessed and rewarded by God. The believer who plays with sex, takes it lightly, and compromises God's principles opens up a Pandora's box that floods his life with a wave of evils he never imagined. Those who try to get the best of both worlds end up with the worst.

Scripture doesn't deny sin's attractiveness or its pleasures. It simply says those pleasures are fleeting, while their consequences stick like glue. Viewed from the long haul, sin is always a raw deal.

Words to the Wise

After warning his son not to lust after an immoral woman, Solomon asked two rhetorical questions:

> Can a man scoop fire into his lap
>   without his clothes being burned?
> Can a man walk on hot coals
>   without his feet being scorched?
>   (Proverbs 6:27-28)

The obvious answer is no—consequences are inescapable. In case the point of the illustrations was missed, Solomon brings it home:

> So is he who sleeps with another man's wife;
> no one who touches her will go unpunished.
> (Proverbs 6:29)

There is no disparity here between the Testaments. The New sounds the same warning as the Old, directed right at believers: "God will judge the adulterer" (Hebrews 13:4).

Throughout Proverbs a special emphasis is placed on the consequences of sexual sin:

> For the lips of an adulteress drip honey,
> and her speech is smoother than oil;
> but in the end she is bitter as gall,
> sharp as a double-edged sword.
> Her feet go down to death;
> her steps lead straight to the grave.
> (Proverbs 5:3-5)

The alluring centerfold, or Internet image, packaged to sell, is Satan's bait. She's the glossy tabloid equivalent of the same adulteress Solomon spoke of centuries ago:

> I find more bitter than death
> the woman who is a snare,
> whose heart is a trap
> and whose hands are chains.
> The man who pleases God will escape her,
> but the sinner she will ensnare.
> (Ecclesiastes 7:26)

Not Just Wrong But Stupid

A friend and I had to confront a man we dearly loved who was living a lie. At one point my friend said to him, "What you're doing is wrong. And it's not only wrong, it's just plain stupid!" He was right. In God's moral universe, governed by the law of the harvest, whatever is right is smart and whatever is wrong is stupid.

> But a man who commits adultery lacks judgment;
>> whoever does so destroys himself.
> Blows and disgrace are his lot,
>> and his shame will never be wiped away.
>> (Proverbs 6:32-33)

Proverbs is a book written by a father for his son. It reminds us that we need not only tell our children to obey God because it's right, but also because it's smart. Sometimes we can all be motivated by smart and stupid when we're not motivated by right and wrong. "You may be sure that your sin will find you out," Moses warned (Numbers 32:23). Sometimes this judgment of God will come only after we have left this world. More often, though, it touches us in this life as well.

Biblical Examples of Immorality's Consequences

The Bible contains numerous examples of sexual sin and its consequences. Genesis records sexual sin in the lives of the people of Sodom (19:1-29), Lot and his daughters (19:30-38), Shechem (34:1-31), Reuben (35:22), Judah and Tamar (38:1-26), and Potiphar's wife (39:1-20).

Consider the consequences of these sexual sins. Sodom and Gomorrah were obliterated by God's judgment. The incest of Lot and his daughters produced two nations: the Moabites and the Ammonites, wicked people who plagued Israel for many generations. Revenge on Shechem's rape of Dinah resulted in the murder of every man in his city. The sins of Reuben and Judah brought shame to the house of Jacob. The uncontrolled lust of Potiphar's wife sent Joseph, an innocent man, to prison.

Samson was God's man of the hour, but his lust after beautiful but unrighteous women led directly to his tragic downfall (Judges 14-16). Not only Samson but his entire nation suffered because he satisfied his desires rather than obeying God.

David was a godly man but 2 Samuel 11 documents the lust that brought him catastrophe. What began as relief from boredom ended in adultery. Actually, it didn't end there. David attempted to circumvent the consequences of his adultery—to cheat the law of the harvest—by covering up. In doing so his sin of adultery expanded to the murder of a righteous man and the death of David's infant son.

David's model of immorality was not lost on his family. When David's son Amnon lusted for his half-sister Tamar, he took what he wanted, just as his father had. This prompted Absalom's murder of Amnon, followed by David's banishment of Absalom. That in turn led to the bitterness that divided David and Absalom and eventually divided the nation.

The final blow was the death of Absalom, for whom David grieved inconsolably (2 Samuel 18:33). Three sons dead, his daughter raped, his family name disgraced. David fulfilled his own words by paying for his sins four times over (2 Samuel 12:6). Like falling dominoes, each toppling the next, immoral choices set into motion a self-perpetuating chain of devastating events.

True to form, even Solomon, the son in whom David put most hope, eventually let his devotion stray from God to ungodly women. In trying to please his seven hundred wives and three hundred concubines, Solomon built altars to their false gods and brought divine judgment on himself and all Israel (1 Kings 11: 1-13).

Sometimes God's judgment on sexual sin is immediate and obvious. Paul warned the Corinthians to learn from the example of Israel in Moses' day: "We should not commit sexual immorality, as some of them did—and in one day twenty-three thousand of them died" (1 Corinthians 10:8). When twenty-three thousand people in one place are struck dead for sexual sin (among other things), the message is not a subtle one.

The Physical Consequences of Sexual Sin

Traditionally, books on Christian morality have stressed heavily the possible physical consequences of sexual sin, specifically unwanted pregnancy and venereal disease. Yet these are not the fundamental reasons for abstaining from extramarital sex. Pregnancy can often be avoided through birth control, and most sexually transmitted diseases, while serious, can be medically treated, though AIDS is a killer of hugh proportions. Still neither pregnancy nor venereal diseases are sins and they never have been. They are only possible consequences. Immorality is the sin.

How many people have acted immorally but have been fortunate enough or, worse yet, deliberate enough to have avoided pregnancy and STDs? Some frown at the pregnant unmarried teenager while smiling at the wonderful young couple in the youth group who, unknown to anyone, behind closed doors are using contraceptives or have had an abortion. (Admire the unwed mother for her courage and help her if she needs it—she did not have to carry that child.)

Pregnancy and STDs are only possible consequences of immorality. Avoiding them while committing immorality may demonstrate foresight, but certainly not morality.

Mental and Emotional Consequences of Sexual Sin

Amnon thought he was deeply in love with Tamar. Yet what he thought was love turned to bitter hatred and disgust after he had raped her (2 Samuel 13:15). Lust, disguising itself as love, often reflects disdain, not commitment, once it is gratified. Many young girls who have sexually surrendered to their boyfriends have learned the "Amnon effect" the hard way. Promises of lifelong love and commitment flow freely in the heat of passion, but often turn to indifference and even contempt.

One afternoon I spoke to a large class of high school seniors in a public school. "Why should I stop having sex with my boyfriend?" asked one girl. "He loves me, and I know he'll marry me."

"How do you know that?" I replied. I shared from experience and research that a high percentage of engagements are broken off, and the majority of people who consider themselves practically engaged do not end up marrying each other. Even the term "premarital sex" is a misnomer because it assumes marriage will take place (either to this person or another). Often it does not.

"But even if he does marry you, will he be faithful?" I asked. "Obviously, he believes in sex outside of marriage. Otherwise he wouldn't go to bed with you now. If he doesn't limit sex to marriage now, what makes you think he will once the two of you are married? Will you ever be able to really trust him, or he you?"

Another consequence of sexual sin is the comparison trap. In a sense we are programmed with each sexual encounter. A man may remember a partner who was more sexually aggressive or more physically attractive. A woman may remember a man who was more sensitive or had a better physique. Comparison can be deadly.

My wife and I are indescribably thankful that we have no one to compare each other to as sexual partners. Couples who marry as virgins have much to be grateful for. Those who have come to Christ from morally loose backgrounds will usually be quick to say the same.

Immorality permanently taints some people's view of sex. Their first sexual encounters came in the back seat of a car or on a living room couch, where both hearts fluttered every time the wind blew or the door rattled. In such cases, sex may be inseparably linked to feelings of fear and guilt. Eventually, some who choose to engage in sex outside marriage cannot enjoy it inside marriage.

Extramarital sex leads to shallow relationships. The focus is on the body, not the real person. Sexual involvement produces more sweat, but less conversation. One disillusioned young man told me of his relationship with a girl: "I wanted something meaningful, but all I got was sex."

Many young people try to prove their love by sexual surrender. But when a relationship has no more unexplored dimensions, boredom usually sets in, along with loss of respect. Sexual compromise is the surest way to end a good relationship. Ironically, it is also an effective way to prolong a bad relationship—many people end up marrying the wrong person because of their sexual involvement (a disastrous consequence that affects the rest of their lives).

The Spiritual Consequences of Immorality

While the physical consequences of immorality may be circumvented, the spiritual consequences are inevitable. Antibiotics will prevent or cure some venereal diseases. Contraceptives will lower the chances of pregnancy. Abortion is a way out of an unwanted pregnancy. But there is no contraceptive for the conscience, and there is no escaping the fact that abortion kills a child. No scientific or medical breakthrough ever changes the fact that I will answer to God for my moral choices. Medical science may eliminate some consequences of my sin, but it cannot remove my accountability to God.

It was to religious people that God said,

"When you spread out your hands in prayer,
   I will hide my eyes from you;
even if you offer many prayers,
   I will not listen" (Isaiah 1:15).

When the adulterous people of Israel sought God, they would not find Him, he said, for He would withdraw Himself from them (Hosea 5:6). Similar statements are found throughout the Old Testament.

To those living in immorality, here is the message: Husband, don't bother praying at meals—God isn't listening. Wife, don't lead out in prayer at a women's Bible study—God won't hear you. Young couple, don't pray that God will bless the wedding ceremony—His ears are deaf to you. Pastor, don't ask God's anointing on Sunday's sermon. If you are living in sexual sin, there is one prayer He is waiting for—the prayer of sincere confession and repentance. He longs for you to start fresh with Him again.

"I wanted to pray that I could share the Gospel with my friend. But I knew God wouldn't hear me because of what I was doing." This young man was having sex with his girlfriend. Without knowing the Scripture quoted above, he sensed his prayers were being blocked by his sin. He was right. By the grace of God he repented, and God was once again pleased to hear and answer.

Our sexual lives cannot be isolated from our spiritual lives. The believers in Corinth tried to separate the two. They still participated in the idolatry and immorality they grew up with and thought they could somehow remain spiritually unaffected by it. Paul told them they were wrong (1 Corinthians 6:12-20; 10:14-22). God is concerned with what I do with my body, for it is the temple of my spirit—and His.

The Effects of Sexual Sin upon Family and Church

We would like to think that if our sexual sin has consequences, at least we alone will bear them. But this is not the case.

No doubt some resented the fact that one man, Achan, caused thirty-six men to die because of his sin (Joshua 7:1-26).

Perhaps some questioned, too, why his whole family was put to death for that sin. We may not understand why, but surely we must learn the lesson that the sins of one can bring terrible consequences on others.

Cindy was twelve years old when her father, a church leader active in evangelism, committed adultery with a woman in the church (his wife's best friend) and left his family. Deeply hurt, Cindy's godly mother remarried hastily and unwisely. In fact, she married a non-Christian.

The scandal was well known throughout the small community, and Cindy had to live with looks of pity and scorn whenever she walked through town. Though a Christian today, Cindy has been through a long series of bad relationships with men, including repeated sexual compromises. Though she is fully responsible for her actions, she is also reaping what her father sowed (Exodus 20:5).

A man formerly active in Christian work resigned because of his homosexual activities. I asked him, "What could have been said to you that might have prevented your first involvement in homosexuality?" After carefully thinking he said, "If someone could have helped me envision the tragedy it would bring to my ministry and the disgrace it would bring to Christ's name, I might never have done it. I have forfeited great ministry opportunities that may never come my way again."

Every church, every Christian organization that harbors sin, sexual or otherwise, simply cannot experience the fullness of God's blessing. "A little yeast works through the whole batch of dough" says Paul (1 Corinthians 5:6). His command to the entire Corinthian Church was to remove the man guilty of sexual sin lest his presence contaminate others in the body as well as bring them all under God's judgment.

The Effects of Sexual Sin on the World

Perhaps there is no more tragic consequence to the sexual sin of Christians than its effect on non-Christians. Nathan said to David, in the wake of his sexual sin, "by doing this you have made the enemies of the LORD show utter contempt . . ." (2 Samuel 12:14).

Nonbelievers, both the sincere and the insincere, look at immorality among Christians and simply conclude that we are hypocrites, no different than the rest of the world. Sometimes, unfortunately, they are right.

While God is working to bring people to Christ through the love and holiness of his people, Satan will do all in his power to rob the Church of her purity and consequently of her effective witness to the watching world. We are on Satan's hit list targeted for immorality. He has strategies to take us down, because if does, he can discredit our Lord in the world's eyes. Only when the people of God confess and repent will they have a credible and effective witness to nonbelievers in the world (Psalm 51:10-13).

CONCLUSION

We should remember that there is no such thing as a private moment. We are on center stage. God is the audience of one. Ultimately we cannot get away with anything.

If we would only rehearse in advance the consequences of immorality, we would be far less prone to commit it.

When I turned eighteen, my friends threw a surprise birthday party for me. They gave me two cakes, covered with delicious frosting and beautiful decorations. But when I was given the knife to cut them, reality set in. I had been deceived. What appeared to be mouthwatering cakes turned out to be two Sears catalogs covered with frosting.

The gift was not what it seemed. In that case it was funny. But when we fall for Satan's lies about sex, there is nothing funny about it. This world is filled with disillusioned and bitter people who have run into a brick wall at the end of a dark alley marked "Sexual Freedom." Despite our rationale for violating God's will, the law of the harvest stands—what we plant, we will reap.

But we must never forget that the law of the harvest applies as much to the rewards of righteousness as to the consequences of sin. If we plant sexual purity today—difficult though it be—in another season, both in this world and the one to come, we will reap a rich harvest.

CHAPTER 10

Forgiveness for Sexual Sin

"**M**ore than anything, I want to feel clean. I want to *be* clean," Terry sighed.

Terry was raised in a Christian home. But for twenty of his forty years he'd lived a life of homosexual promiscuity with hundreds of sexual partners.

The good news is that people like Terry—people like you and me—can be clean. Forgiveness and moral cleansing come from asking and accepting Christ's provision for our sin.

Jesus and Sexual Sinners

Jesus loved and forgave sexual sinners. The gospels take pains to tell us that. He lived in a culture that mercilessly stigmatized immoral women. Branded as sinners of the worst kind, these women carried a life-long scarlet letter. Yet Jesus reached out and touched their lives, among them the Samaritan woman of John 4, the adulterous woman of John 8, and the immoral woman of Luke 7.

"Neither do I condemn you," he said to the adulterous woman. "Go now and leave your life of sin" (John 8:11).

Of the immoral but repentant woman, Jesus said, "Her many sins have been forgiven—for she loved much. But he who has been forgiven little loves little." "Your sins are forgiven," he assured her. "Your faith has saved you; go in peace" (Luke 7:47-50).

Sexual sin is serious, but it is not beyond Jesus' grace and power to forgive. He outraged the chief priests and elders by telling them, "the prostitutes are entering the kingdom of God ahead of you" (Matthew 21:31).

Jesus not only forgives sexual sin, He understands sexual temptation:

> For we do not have a high priest who is unable to sympathize with our weaknesses, but we have one who has been tempted in every way, just as we are—yet was without sin. Let us then approach the throne of grace with confidence, so that we may receive mercy and find grace to help us in our time of need (Hebrews 4:15-16).

How Much Can God Forgive?

The parable of the unmerciful servant (Matthew 18:21-35) teaches us two things about sin: first, it is infinitely beyond our capacity to repay, and second, it is infinitely greater than any offense we have suffered—or could suffer—at the hands of others. Without a penetrating perspective of ourselves as impoverished sinners, we cannot appreciate God's grace and cannot truly forgive others as we should.

The forgiveness of God is a prominent theme throughout Scripture, one that should invoke from us expressions of wonder and praise. I cite here a single passage from each testament. There are countless others.

> The LORD is compassionate and gracious,
>   slow to anger, abounding in love.
> He will not always accuse,
>   nor will he harbor his anger forever;
> he does not treat us as our sins deserve
>   or repay us according to our iniquities.
> For as high as the heavens are above the earth,
>   so great is his love for those who fear him;
> as far as the east is from the west,
>   so far has he removed our transgressions from us.
> As a father has compassion on his children,
>   so the LORD has compassion on those who fear him;
> for he knows how we are formed,
>   he remembers that we are dust.
>   (Psalm 103:8-14)

What, then, shall we say in response to this? If God is for us, who can be against us? He who did not spare his own Son, but gave him up for us all—how will he not also, along with him, graciously give us all things? Who will bring any charge against those whom God has chosen? It is God who justifies. Who is he that condemns? Christ Jesus, who died—more than that, who was raised to life—is at the right hand of God and is also interceding for us. Who shall separate us from the love of Christ? Shall trouble or hardship or persecution or famine or nakedness or danger or sword? . . . No, in all these things we are more than conquerors through him who loved us. For I am convinced that neither death nor life, neither angels nor demons, neither the present nor the future, nor any powers, neither height nor depth, nor anything else in all creation, will be able to separate us from the love of God that is in Christ Jesus our Lord (Romans 8:31-39).

What is the bottom line of God's forgiveness? He has seen me at my worst and still loves me; because He knows everything I've ever thought or done, there are no skeletons in my closet; His love for me cannot be earned and, therefore, cannot be lost; I am totally secure in His unconditional work of grace for me.

Christ not only removes my condemnation and considers me innocent, he declares me righteous. I am as acceptable, yes *commendable*, to the Father as Christ Himself (2 Corinthians 5:21). God is totally and irreversibly satisfied with me because he is totally and irreversibly satisfied with Christ's work on my behalf (1 John 2:2; 4:10).

Paul gave the Corinthians this bad news:

Neither the sexually immoral nor idolaters, nor adulterers nor male prostitutes nor homosexual offenders nor thieves nor the greedy nor drunkards nor slanderers nor swindlers will inherit the kingdom of God (1 Corinthians 6:9-10).

But he didn't stop there:

And that is what some of you were. But you were washed, you were sanctified, you were justified in the name of the Lord Jesus Christ and by the Spirit of our God (6:11).

This is a matter of transformed identity—in Christ. We are no longer who we used to be. "Therefore, if anyone is in Christ, he is a new creation; the old has gone, the new has come!" (2 Corinthians 5:17). I am Christ's bride, clothed in "fine linen, bright and clean" (Revelation 19:7-8). *Clean*—the very thing Terry, my tired and defeated homosexual friend, longed to be.

Then What about the Consequences?

One of the hardest questions we face is how to reconcile two paradoxical scriptural principles: forgiveness for sin and having to live with the consequences of sin. We must face the fact that the Bible clearly teaches both, and we must believe both even if we do not understand how they can both be true.

Christ took upon Himself the *ultimate* consequences of my sin—eternal death. This I will never have to experience. But the unpleasant fact remains that in this life there are still consequences for some of the very sins He has removed from me.

If I drank a bottle of wine, got in my car, drove seventy miles an hour in the rain, and hit and killed a ten-year-old girl on her bicycle, would God forgive me if I repented? Of course. Would his forgiveness bring the girl back to life? Of course not. Nor would it save me from prosecution or imprisonment.

Christ's blood cleanses us from sin's guilt, but it does not remove all of sin's consequences. God can forgive me for premarital sex, but I can never be a virgin again. God can forgive me for a homosexual relationship, but I might still die from AIDS.

Being forgiven doesn't change our accountability for what we've done. Repentance doesn't alter the laws of biology that affect pregnancy, the forces that cause venereal disease, or even (automatically) the emotional trauma related to guilt. God may supernaturally remove these things if He chooses, and no doubt He sometimes does. It appears that far more often, however, He does not.

Forgiveness of sin is real. Consequences for sin are also real. Neither invalidates the other.

Whenever I teach this concept, I invariably receive some strong negative reactions. No matter how I stress forgiveness, people become upset, thinking I am saying Christ's blood is not enough to take away our sins.

In a Bible college class, several students were vigorously arguing with me that forgiveness is not *really* forgiveness if any consequences still have to be faced. One elderly lady in the class raised her hand and rescued me (possibly from being stoned!). Speaking in a hoarse and raspy voice, she said, "For forty years I smoked three packs of cigarettes a day. When I became a Christian ten years ago, I stopped. Call it a sin or just a bad habit, Christ forgave me for it and I gave it up. But listen to my voice. And take my word for it, my lungs are black. I have no trouble at all understanding that we have to live with some consequences, even after God forgives us."

But don't I pay for my sins when I face consequences for them?

No, not in any redemptive sense. Christ went to Hell for us on the cross; He does not want us to go through Hell later or now. He is there to help us face the natural consequences of our sin and even enrich us through them.

Mary, a Christian woman who committed adultery, said: "What I've done is too bad to expect forgiveness. Certainly my husband can't forgive me, and I don't believe God can either. I must suffer for it myself. There is no other way."

Mary knew her Bible—but she did not understand it. To live in a self-imposed purgatory or to inflict it on others says Christ's work is insufficient and implies a worthiness and capacity of our own to pay off our debt. Attempts at self-atonement are as prideful as they are pitiful.

Mary is still living in a prison, groaning under her captivity, yet all the while holding in her hand the key (Christ's redemptive work) to unlock the chains and bars that hold her. As for her sexual sin, her refusal to accept Christ's forgiveness will not give her strength to avoid it. Far more likely, it will prompt her to repeat it.

Many believers are like Mary, laboring under such guilt that they "unconsciously arrange their lives—even to the point of choosing poor marriage partners or unworthy occupations—so they can punish themselves."[1]

Christ paid the debt for our sins. He did it once and He did it right. We must accept His atonement, not try to repeat it.

Living with Our Failures

How can we live with ourselves when we have sinned against God and failed to live pure lives? First, by realizing that growth is often achieved through picking up the pieces after we have miserably failed. Scripture does not say a righteous man never falls. It does say "though a righteous man falls seven times, he rises again" (Proverbs 24:16). Whenever we fall we have opportunity to learn a lesson about the sufficiency of Christ. Self-sufficiency is the great enemy of faith. Failure is the great enemy of self-sufficiency.

Some of the healthiest people are former heart attack victims. Because they took their heart attacks seriously, they began to eat right, exercise regularly, and live as healthy lives as possible. Some of them are accomplished marathon runners. Many will long outlive their friends who never experienced their trauma—and were therefore never shaken into changing their lives.

Likewise, some of the most spiritual people I know once lived in immorality. There is forgiveness, deliverance, and new life for anyone, regardless of his or her background. In fact, God views such backgrounds as opportunities to display the extent of His grace and life-changing power.

A Warning to the Presumptuous

Those who understand God's grace understand that this does not mean we should seek to fall into sin—"Shall we go on sinning so that grace may increase? By no means! We died to sin; how can we live in it any longer?" (Romans 6:1-2). The grace of God should never lead to presumption, indifference, or dropping our guard against temptation. In fact, it should have the opposite effect (Titus 2:11-12).

Not only does sin have consequences, but each time we sin we reinforce a pattern that becomes harder and harder to break. If we persist in sin with the thought that one day we will get right with God, we should remind ourselves that God may still be there to forgive and restore . . . but we may not be.

What About Guilt Feelings?

More and more Christians are adopting the position of secular psychologists (who are occasionally right, of course) that all guilt feelings are harmful. Whether or not this is true depends on one's definitions of "guilt" and "guilt feelings."

In one sense, only those with a seared or desensitized conscience never feel any guilt. Mass murderers, for instance, sometimes have no guilt feelings at all. Obviously, an absence of guilt feelings is no guarantee of spiritual or mental health.

There is what *could* be called a feeling of guilt that often accompanies the convicting work of the Holy Spirit. It is a sorrow for true guilt (unrighteousness) that leads to repentance (2 Corinthians 7:9). Whether or not this should be called a guilt feeling is not all that important. What is important is that there is such a thing as true moral guilt (as many secular psychologists do not acknowledge), and that guilt must be somehow perceived in order to be dealt with. We should, therefore, be grateful for a guilt feeling *if* it does, in fact, stem from true guilt, *if* it flows from a mental perception of that guilt, *if* it prompts us to take the God-given measures to deal with that guilt, and *if* it subsides once the true guilt is removed.

David expresses deep feelings of guilt (Psalm 32:3-5; 51:3-4) and attributes them to the heavy hand of God leading him to confession, repentance, and a fresh start.

Two common kinds of guilt feelings, however, are tragic—those rooted in true moral guilt, yet not leading to confession, repentance, and freedom from the guilt and its accompanying feelings, and guilt feelings stemming from false guilt.

Motivator or Demotivator?

Often children who have been sexually abused, especially in incestuous relationships, feel overwhelmingly guilty. Some people feel guilty just for struggling with sexual temptation, which itself is not sin. An adolescent may be consumed with out-of-proportion guilt because he seems unable to stop masturbating. Some people feel guilty about everything—and are spiritually paralyzed because of it.

Unresolved guilt feelings are demotivating. A coach who demeans and belittles doesn't bring out the best in most of us. On the contrary, he makes us feel like quitting. Likewise, residual guilt feelings (those left after confession and forgiveness) do not inspire us to better behavior, but to worse.

Discouragement never fosters accomplishment. The cycle of defeat in many Christians is as predictable as it is devastating: we fail, feel guilty, try to offset our guilt by making new resolutions, then fail again and feel more guilty than ever. After the cycle repeats itself again and again, many of us just give up. "Why try anymore when you know you'll fail?" The result is an endless vortex in which we love God, but trust God too little, and hate ourselves, but trust ourselves too much.

Like a dark cloud, guilt feelings hover over us, sapping us of spiritual energy. False guilt feelings, or guilt not dealt with, can drive us to depression and suicide, and more often to a paralysis of the will that results in a defeated Christian life.

What to Do When I Sin

What steps should I take in order to deal with sin? First, *I must admit my sin to myself*. I need to call sin sin, not just a mistake or a little slip, and quit rationalizing and making excuses. Jesus died for our sins, not our excuses for our sins.

Second, *I must confess my sin to God.* Since He knows about it already, the purpose is not to inform Him. It is to verbally agree with God that what I have done is, in fact, sin.

Third, as a part of my admission and confession, *I must genuinely repent.* True confession is not a begrudging or flippant admission of wrongdoing, but an expression of guilt, regret, and desire and intention to change. I've had people tell me they were sorry for adultery, yet refuse to quit seeing their partner in adultery. Actually, their sorrow is for sin's consequences, not for sin. They *admitted* something—but they confessed nothing.

Finally, there is a place in the family and church to *confess my sins not only to God but to others* (James 5:16). Two cautions should be exercised in such confession: first, it is made to those who have actually been hurt by the behavior (this may or may not include a whole church body), and second, details should be shared only as necessary. God has no problem forgetting the details, but people do. Why etch on their minds images that will be hard or impossible to shake?

I believe adultery is a sin that should be confessed to one's partner, but I have seen husbands and wives share details of adulterous relationships that left vivid pictures, deepened wounds, and increased bitterness. I know one pastor who took a young woman from his church out to lunch to confess—and ask her forgiveness for—his lustful thoughts toward her. Embarrassed, but flattered, within a month the girl was having an affair with him. Unwise and undiscerning confession dishonors God and may actually compound the problem.

Forgive Others

If we have admitted, confessed, and repented of our sin, we have been forgiven by God whether or not we feel like it. But there is yet another dimension and evidence of forgiveness. If we have experienced God's forgiveness, it will be shown in our forgiveness of others. In the parable of the unmerciful servant, Jesus teaches that forgiving others is part and parcel of our own forgiveness (Matthew 18:21-35).

"You must forgive to be forgiven" is a foreign concept to many believers. Strange, since it is clearly assumed in the most often repeated passage in Scripture, the Lord's Prayer: "Forgive us our debts, as we also have forgiven our debtors" (Matthew 6:12). In fact, this is apparently the central emphasis of the prayer, for it is the only aspect Christ elaborates on in the following verses:

> For if you forgive men when they sin against you, your heavenly Father will also forgive you. But if you do not forgive men their sins, your Father will not forgive your sins (Matthew 6:14-15).

"But how can I forgive my wife for committing adultery?" "How can I forgive my fiancé for pressuring me into premarital sex?" "How can I forgive my father for molesting me?" Without a doubt, sexual sins are among the hardest to forgive, but clearly they are not an exception to Christ's rule of forgiveness.

I have seen great miracles of rebuilding when one partner has truly forgiven the other's adultery, and bitter tragedies when forgiveness was not sought or sought but not received. One of the most powerful miracles occurred when a thirty-

year-old woman went back to her father and told him she forgave him for sexually abusing her when she was a child.

Forgiveness is a matter of choice, not feelings. Yes, we may
remember the facts, but we must not allow ourselves to dwell
on them. The offense must be buried in the past and not
exhumed in the present. It is possible to "forgive and forget" if
we truly do forgive. But we will never forget what we choose
to brood over, and if we brood over it, we demonstrate we
have not truly forgiven.

We must refuse to cater to our emotions or indulge our
fatal tendency toward bitterness. We must not simply suppress
resentment but confess it as sin. "Time heals all wounds" is an
erroneous maxim. If we do not rehearse others' offenses, if we
do not indulge our vengeful tendencies, then time will bring
healing. But time never heals the cancer of bitterness—it only
allows it to grow.

"Can we really forgive those who continue in sin?" We
should never excuse them, defend them, or guard them from
the consequences of their sin. We can't always eliminate our
pain. But we can release them—and ourselves—from our bitterness or resentment.

Forgiveness is not unrealistic. A woman whose husband
continues over a period of time in unrepentant adultery is not
to pretend nothing is happening. She might take steps that
include separating herself and the children from him.
Certainly, she must let him see that continued sin will take its
toll. To whitewash his sin hurts him as much as herself and the
children. She should forgive him "seventy times seven," but
that does not mean that when he continually rips the fabric of
their marriage that she will be a party to his sin by keeping up
the front of an unbroken home.

It *does* mean, however, that she will pray for his repentance and offer restoration if it comes. It also means that—realizing she cannot control him and he will answer not to her but to God—she will surrender to God her claim on his life. Even if he never repents and she never lives with him again, she is called upon to offer him forgiveness. It is painful yet possible for us to forgive the worst offenses.

Moving on from Past Sins

"I wish I'd wake up and the nightmare would be over. I wish so much I'd never been unfaithful." Helen was sincere. But, like many of us, she needed to leave her past—and the sin of her past—and move on. Once confessed and repented of, sin should be put behind us.

When I was a boy, I had a golden retriever named Champ. Whenever we gave him a bone, he'd chew it till it was bare, then take off to bury it. But once it was buried, he would never let it lie. Every day, sometimes several times a day, he would make his rounds, going to every buried bone—dozens of them—and digging them up to chew on some more. Then he'd bury them again, only to repeat the process till the day he died.

Unlike my dog, God buries our sins and lets them lie; He never digs them up (Micah 7:18-19). Like my dog, however, sometimes we do. We dig up old sins, chew on them, confess them again, and bury them—but in a shallow grave whose location we memorize for convenient access. We do this not only to ourselves, but others. We piously say "I forgive you," but dig up old sins to chew on at our pity parties, wave in front of others as gossip, or use as weapons of revenge or tools to barter and manipulate. In doing so, we become obsessed with sin instead of the Savior. We give more credit to its power than to His.

Once confessed, sins should be forgotten. We should choose to dwell on them no longer:

> Forgetting what is behind and straining toward what is ahead, I press on toward the goal to win the prize for which God has called me heavenward in Christ Jesus (Philippians 3:13-14).

Chapter 10, Notes

1. Bruce Narramore and Bill Counts, *Freedom from Guilt* (Eugene, Ore.: Harvest House Publishers, 1974), 12.

PART 4

What Can We Do to Promote Sexual Purity?

CHAPTER 11

Restoring Sexual Sanity

The individual believer needs to remove sources of sexual temptation, avoid temptation, and run from temptation—"flee from sexual immorality" (1 Corinthians 6:18). When he cannot remove it, avoid it, or run from it (usually he can), he must dig in his heels, call upon the purity of his new identity in Christ (Colossians 3:1-14) and the power of the indwelling Spirit, and stand firm with his God-given armor, wielding "the sword of the Spirit, which is the word of God" (Ephesians 6:17). All this he must do quickly, since it is most true of sexual temptation that "he who hesitates is lost."

No one can become prepared for such a battle on short notice. Prior to the confrontation the mind must have been exposed to God's Word, and the life planted in a climate of spiritual growth that includes Bible study, prayer, and Christian fellowship. The believer who isolates sexual temptation from the whole of his life in Christ is doomed to failure.

There are a few books that deal with sexual temptation, and many that deal with temptation in general. Some of these offer help to the individual Christian. Too often, however, the believer is addressed as just that—an individual. He is seen as fending for himself in the sexual wilderness, isolated from the major formers and reinforcers of identity—his family, his church, and his society.

In this chapter we will examine what the family and Church can do for the believer to cultivate his sexual purity, and what believers together can do for the sexual moral welfare of our society.

WHAT WE CAN DO IN THE FAMILY

When my daughters were two and four, I took them out for breakfast at a restaurant. On the way back to the car, I was surprised to see they both had toothpicks in their mouths. Reaching to my mouth, I found I too had a toothpick. Unconsciously, I had picked it up at the counter after paying. It's a habit, something I always do, but never think about. And almost as second naturedly as I, my little girls—who didn't even know what a toothpick was for—imitated my action.

There, in miniature, is parenthood. Children pick up on everything we do, consciously or unconsciously. Sometimes it's amusing. Sometimes it's scary.

As one family watched television together, an immoral scene came on the screen. Being good Christian parents, Mom and Dad asked the children to leave the room (that is, unfortunately, more than many parents would do). But they themselves kept watching. What lesson did the children learn?

"I can't watch garbage, but Mom and Dad can. When I grow up, I can watch garbage too because garbage is okay for big people."

A Christian father can say "Sex outside of marriage is wrong," but when his son sees him leering at a woman at the beach or on television or in a magazine, a whole different value system is taught—the parent's real value system, not the one he professes. What we *do* speaks so loudly that our children can't hear what we're saying. Sometimes our children may fail to listen to us. Rarely will they fail to *imitate* us.

Develop a Strong Marriage

The quality of your family life will not rise above the quality of your marriage. The greatest sexual legacy you can give your children is to show them a good marriage, to daily demonstrate loyal love for your spouse. My wife excels at this. She is always building me up in our children's eyes, showing respect and appreciation for me, as I do for her. This is never lost on the children.

Good cross-sexual relationships build good cross-sexual relationships. It's hard for a teenage girl to know what to look for in a guy when she (and most likely her mother) doesn't respect her dad.

Make improving your marriage a project. Buy one of the myriad of good books on communication and strengthening your marriage. Attend a Family Life Conference* or Marriage Encounter weekend. Ask your pastor's help in strengthening your marriage.

*Contact 1-800-358-6329 (FLToday)

Spend time together alone. Go out on dates. Put each other in your appointment books. Have someone you trust watch your children, then focus on each other for the evening. Communicate. Share the little things and the big. Take an interest in each other's day. Talk about God. Read Scripture together. Pray together. Share your needs, your joys and sorrows, frustrations, plans and dreams.

When you're experiencing this kind of intimacy, it spills over into every facet of the family. It creates a climate in the home that is a tribute to sexual (male-female) relationships.

Being affectionate with your spouse not only expresses and enhances your intimacy, it teaches your children how special the ultimate male-female relationship can be. It says "touching is good," and "touching in marriage is the most special of all." Obviously, discretion is important. But your children need to see that affection flows out of commitment—that physical intimacy and marriage are two sides of the same coin despite what the rest of the world is telling them.

The husband and wife's sexual relationship is important as a cultivator of intimacy *and* a guard against immorality. That's why Paul says to the married: "Do not cheat each other of normal sexual intercourse" (1 Corinthians 7:5, Phillips).

Train Your Children

Both Testaments make clear the parental responsibility to train children in the way of righteousness (Deuteronomy 6:1-9; Ephesians 6:4). Parents should first of all seek to cultivate a love and devotion to God in their children. Second, they should train them in moral principles, especially the principles of choice and consequence, wisdom and folly. In

Proverbs, Solomon teaches his son practical moral principles including guidelines for sexual purity.

Children should be taught correct values, how to recognize conflicting values, and how to resist the temptations they present. They should be taught to value the inner person, not just the outer. First Peter 3:1-6 suggests mothers need to teach their daughters a great deal more than how to look in a mirror, put on makeup, and win the attention of boys.

> Charm is deceptive, and beauty is fleeting;
>> but a woman who fears the Lord is to be praised.
>> (Proverbs 31:30)

We need to put less emphasis on projecting images and more on cultivating character. Beauty is easily lost; character is an investment in eternity.

Children should be taught to love righteousness and hate sin. Too often Christian families declare a truce with sin and live in a state of detente—tolerating unrighteousness and letting it gradually claim more and more territory in the home.

The kind of clothing worn by children is the responsibility of their parents, especially the father. Any man will tell you that the current crop of women's swimsuits communicates only one thing to men—regardless of a woman's motives in wearing them. There will be some years that for the sake of sexual purity, mother's and daughter's swimsuits—and perhaps father's and son's—will have to be out of style. Children are trained by the clothing their parents allow and encourage them to wear.

One of the greatest assets you can pass on to your child is self-control. If he does not learn it from you at an early age, when he's older he may never carry on the holy habits of Bible study, prayer, and church attendance. Without self-control, he will find it exceptionally difficult to resist temptations, sexual and otherwise.

Develop close family relationships. Spend time together. Don't just say your family is priority—*show* them they're priority.

A close family is an accountable family. By loving each other and having fun together, you earn the right to caution, challenge, and confront when you see wrong attitudes and actions. Too many parents descend from Mt. Olympus just long enough to throw a few lightning bolts. The hit and run approach to morally training your children is a disaster.

The Critical Role of the Father

Sexual identity studies clearly show that the father is the parent who most greatly influences the sexual development of the children. If he is absent, indifferent, weak, or hostile, it will adversely affect both his sons' and daughters' sexual identities, in some cases resulting in homosexual tendencies. Often a mother will try to compensate for her husband's hostility or distance from the children, or his lack of leadership, and end up playing a domineering role in the home, further confusing the children's sexual identities and role perceptions.

Christian fathers who find themselves constantly away from home should keep this in mind. Curtailing outside activities, business hours, or even finding another job might free up the critical time your children need to have with you.

When death or divorce leave children without a father, it is important that the children, especially boys, regularly spend time with positive male role models, perhaps a college age boy or man in the church.[1]

Parents should not live under a burden of guilt for the lifestyle choices their grown children have made. Homosexuality is not always as predictable as it might sound. Sometimes parents do a fine job raising their children and it still happens. Nevertheless, homosexuality is certainly much easier to prevent than to correct. If you see signs of or tendencies toward homosexuality in your children, the earlier you deal with them the better.

I know of several cases where parents have been concerned about their child's sexual identity and behavior and were told, both by friends and professionals, "don't be alarmed" and "that's just a passing phase." Too often the passing phase develops into a lifestyle. Certainly not every act of childhood curiosity will lead to sexual perversion. While they should avoid becoming paranoid or overreacting, Christian parents *must* be perceptive to their children's psychosexual development and needs.

The Importance of Modesty

Family modesty is an important part of sex education. By modesty I do not mean a paranoia that faints or screams when a child sees a parent or sibling without clothes on. Modesty is a healthy attitude that says, "My sexual parts are special. God made them that way. They are so special that I respect them by covering them when other people are around . . . just like my mommy and daddy do."

While there is nothing wrong with children seeing their parents and siblings unclothed from time to time at an early age, I recommend that nudity not become a habitual part of family life.

Remember that sex drives exist considerably before puberty. A mother who thinks her son is "just a little boy" might be surprised to know what he's thinking when he sees her naked. The importance of family modesty is intensified by the sad but real problem of temptation toward incestuous relations, especially of brothers toward their sisters and fathers toward their daughters.

Guidelines for Sex Education

Here are some guidelines parents may find helpful in teaching their children about sex:

If you don't know the facts, don't be embarrassed—just find them out. In this sex-saturated culture, everybody thinks we should know everything about sex. But often we don't.

There are many fine resources for Christian parents, including James Dobson's *Preparing for Adolescence*, Mark Laaser's *Talking to Your Kids About Sex,* and Lois Walfrid Johnson's *You Are Wonderfully Made.* Ask your pastor and other parents for advice in what to say and how and when to say it.

Always teach sex in the context of values, responsibility, and marriage. When you teach your children anatomy, don't do it as if their sex organs are parts of a car engine. Relate them to their purpose.

Sex is so much more than biology. It is a matter of ethics and religion as well. If you create a tie between sex and marriage when your children are young, they will find it hard to conceive of sex having a place outside of marriage. And that's exactly as it should be. In contrast, sex education in the schools often isolates sex from its proper spiritual and ethical implications.

Know your child. Some children are sexually precocious; others are not. Some need to hear direct and to the point answers. Others respond better to a more subtle approach. You are the parent—no one is better qualified than you to discern what your child is ready to hear.

Answer your child's questions honestly. This may require some forethought. It is good to anticipate some of the questions that will be coming your way.

One of the classic questions is "Where do babies come from?" or "How does a baby get inside his Mommy's tummy?" To a younger child you might explain it this way: "Mommy and Daddy love each other, so they hold each other close, and sometimes God decides to make a baby—part from Mommy and part from Daddy."

Tell them as much as they need to know now. A five-year-old does not need to see a diagram of sexual intercourse, nor does he need to be told "The baby's in Mommy's uterus, not her tummy." Not every technical error needs to be corrected at an early age. Giving too much information too early may overwhelm a child. Discussing details of sexual intimacy can push a child to "grow up" sexually before his time (a major danger fostered by the media).

On the other hand, an eleven-year-old needs to know a great deal more than a five-year-old. If Mom and Dad don't explain sexual intercourse to him, someone else will very soon (if they haven't already) and probably not in the nicest way.

Still, the eleven-year-old doesn't need to know about matters such as premature ejaculation and birth control. In fact, things such as these would be better learned very shortly before marriage.

Unfortunately, the bombardment of sexual information (and misinformation) is so great that many twelve-year-olds know a great deal about sex. Once a child—whether too young or not—has learned something about sexual relations, parents need to be sure he has the right information and the right perspective.

Don't procrastinate. Too much too soon is one problem. Too little too late is another. It's too easy to wait for the right opportunity that never comes. Sometimes our children have already been misinformed or developed irrational fears about sex, and it's always harder to correct wrong thinking than to prevent it.

Don't try to calculate your child's exact date of puberty, then start telling him about sex the night before. It can be traumatic for boys to ejaculate and not understand what has happened, and even worse for girls to begin menstruating with no or only partial information. By the time some parents get around to telling their children about sex, their children know more than they do.

Remember, it's much easier to tell a twelve-year-old about sex than do what many Christian parents have done—had their first heart-to-heart talk about sex with their pregnant fifteen-year-old.

Don't come on too strong. It's best to spread things out, not dump the whole load of sexual knowledge at once. It's easy to overwhelm children not only with information but with emotions, especially negative ones. Difficult subjects like homosexuality need to be discussed with children as they get older.

But parents must be careful not to sound threatening or angry—they must be calm and remain approachable or their children will repress and hide their sexual questions and struggles for fear of rejection.

Be positive. Some parents tell their children about sex only because they have to. But they are so uncomfortable and tentative that, without meaning to, they communicate, "This is an unpleasant and shady thing we're talking about. I wish I was somewhere else, don't you?"

I know one girl who learned about menstruation through a note from her mother—passed under her bedroom door. This clandestine approach made a strong negative statement about female sexuality.

Protect Your Children Against Sexual Abuse

Sexual abuse of children is alarmingly frequent. Parents must take reasonable precautions to protect their children from such abuse.

Parents should regularly visit their children's schools, especially day-care centers. The same applies to scouts, clubs, and church groups. Parents should insist on their right to visit their children's activities at any time and at any place—and should deliberately make periodic unexpected visits.

Parents should check in on their children's play with each other, monitor their neighborhood activities, and know what goes on when their children are visiting neighbors, friends, and even relatives (the majority of child abusers are relatives).

Children should not be sent alone into public restrooms without reasonable precautions. When they are too young to resist or defend themselves, they should not walk long distances alone. Parents should teach them to resist lures from strangers, such as "Would you like a ride?" "Will you help me find my lost puppy?" "Can I take your picture over there?" and "Want to play a fun game?"

Children should be instructed to allow no one to touch their private parts, undress them, or undress in front of them.

Parents should be aware that father/daughter, stepfather/daughter, and brother/sister incest are the most common forms of sexual child abuse. Mothers must be particularly aware of family relationships. Fathers who struggle with sexual temptation toward their children should get help before they do permanent damage to their children and themselves.

Parents need to be sensitive to sexual abuse clues, including genital pain and rashes, depression, withdrawal, antisocial or regressive behavior, nightmares, and running away from home. Children who say they have been sexually abused should be believed unless and until it is proven otherwise. Studies show that children rarely lie about sexual abuse on their own initiative. Unfortuately they can be pressured or manipulated into making allegations when adults make it clear they want to hear a certain kind of confession.

Exercise Parental Control

There are overwhelming societal pressures on the young and on their parents to regard early sex as inevitable in our social climate.[2]

Parents *must* resist those pressures, or their children never will.

I'm alarmed at how many parents do not want to interfere in their children's lives. I believe most Christian parents today are not overprotective, but underprotective of their children, at least when it comes to understanding and dealing with their developing sexual perceptions, values, and behaviors.

Parents are responsible to see that their children's friends are good influences. "Do not be misled: 'Bad company corrupts good character'" (1 Corinthians 15:33). Peer pressure is incredibly strong. It is our business to know about and provide direction for our children's relationships with others.

Parents are responsible for the school their children attend and what they're learning there. God entrusted your child to you, not the school, whether public or Christian. It is *your* responsibility to see that they are taught what is right.

I've known Christian parents who wish their teenagers wouldn't bring home R-rated movies for their home videos, wish their daughters wouldn't wear suggestive swimsuits and prom dresses, and wish their sons wouldn't tell dirty jokes, put certain posters on their walls, or listen to rock music that glorifies immorality. Christian parents, we need to wake up! We must stop *wishing* and *start* acting! God does not give us responsibility without corresponding authority.

"But I don't want my children to think I don't trust them." Trust is important, but it is never unrealistic. Parents don't trust their children to play on the freeway. It's not a matter of trust, just common sense and wisdom. Some parents trust their teenagers doing things I wouldn't trust myself to do.

Some parents trust their teenager to be in a car alone on a date till 1:00 A.M. Usually this is *neglect*, not trust. It is also the height of naiveté. What did you do when you were in a car with a date at 1:00 A.M.? Chances are, you weren't reciting Bible verses. How soon we forget . . .

"But my teenager is a Christian." Was your teenager born

without glands? When he became a Christian did he develop green blood instead of red? If we parents give our young people this kind of freedom, we need to be prepared to share the responsibility for the powerful sexual temptations they will confront but may not yet be ready to resist.

Psychologist Henry Brandt's son was upset when his father didn't permit him to go out alone in a car with a girl. "What's wrong, Dad? Don't you trust me?"

"In a car—alone at night with a girl?" Brandt replied. "I wouldn't trust me. Why should I trust you?"[3]

Control the TV

The television is a good place to start exercising more positive parental control. Start by keeping a record of every minute each family member (including Mom and Dad) watches television for one whole week. When you add up the total, you may be shocked or embarrassed into watching less.

Decide in advance how much television per week to watch—perhaps eight hours or five selected programs per week. Or choose two days a week when the television can be on, and keep it off on the others. You can decide in advance which programs to watch and stick to the schedule you've determined. This will keep the television from being mindlessly flipped on and your brain flipped off.

"Fasting" from TV for a period of weeks or months helps keep it under control. Just try going a week without television in your home—to remind yourself of how pleasant life can be without it. Some people get rid of their televisions entirely. After the initial withdrawal symptoms, most are relieved and happy at all the time they have to do other things (like relating to each other, calling a friend in need, visiting a neighbor, and other forgotten practices of the pre-TV era). If you keep a TV, try keeping it in your closet. This way, it will take an intelligent effort to go and get it out. Determine to watch only shows that uplift biblical values and turn them off when they don't. Discuss programs as a family. Why is this one good or this one bad? This will develop moral discernment in the whole family. Do *not* allow your children to pick any programs they wish—that is your responsibility.

Beware of using television as a babysitter—especially when the programming doesn't contribute to your child's spiritual and moral development. Provide alternatives for your child, such as reading, projects, and healthy play. Even good TV programs watched too often encourage passivity and discourage meaningful play, interaction, and communication—essential to proper development.

Here's a radical idea—require that you and any family member spend one hour reading the Bible or engaging in ministry for each hour spent watching television. Is it too much to ask that God be given equal time with ABC?

IT'S OUR RESPONSIBILITY

We parents can save ourselves and everyone else a lot of confusion if we recognize our God-given responsibility to teach our children about sex. We cannot and should not expect the schools, the media, or anyone else to do our job for us, even though they will if we don't (and they will try even if we do). Naturally, we'll make mistakes in educating our children about sex. But just giving it a conscious effort will put us far ahead of most parents.

A sixteen-year-old girl spent the evening with our family. We were watching what seemed to be a good television program when a scene came on showing an unmarried couple obviously moving toward sexual intercourse. When I turned it off, she said, "That's not for me. I'm saving myself for my husband—whoever he'll be. My marriage present to him will be me. He'll be my first and only; that's the best I can give him."

I was proud of her. But even more, I was proud of her parents.

WHAT WE CAN DO IN THE CHURCH

The Church is to challenge the world's morality, not mirror it. It is to be an oasis in a spiritual desert. Yet it's increasingly impossible, morally speaking, to tell where the world ends and the Church begins.

Getting Our Heads Out of the Sand

What can the Church do about its moral decline? First, we must be more aware. We can no longer afford to be naive. We must face the fact that beneath the squeaky clean Sunday morning exteriors are many hurting people, more than a few in mental and physical bondage to sexual sin. In too many churches the reality of such problems is ignored. We pretend they don't exist or only exist far away. Unless this changes, the Church is destined to irrelevance, a fate worse than extinction.

Church leaders must realize that the reading and viewing

habits of their people are not very different from those of their non-Christian neighbors. Furthermore, we must stop assuming that everyone in our churches knows what is right and wrong. We need to teach the ABCs of morality. One man and woman from non-Christian backgrounds lived together in fornication for two years while they were regularly involved in an evangelical church. They never tried to cover it up, but not once did they hear the subject dealt with. Church leaders cannot presume people know what the Bible says is right and wrong. We must tell them.

Nor is it enough to tell only the youth groups about sex. Tell their parents. Don't just give junior high and high schoolers guidelines for resisting temptation. Give them to the whole congregation. Lust may begin in adolescence—it certainly doesn't end there!

After I preached several weeks on the subject of sexual purity, one man in our church told me, "Thanks so much. I had come to believe I was the only Christian who ever struggled with lust."

Helping Each Other in God's Family

Churches need to devote men's breakfasts, retreats, and other opportunities to developing camaraderie and accountability in living holy lives. Women's groups need to not only learn Bible content, but how to identify and resist the temptations to transfer their affection from their husbands to other men. The Church's mature women are to teach the younger women to "love their husbands," to "be self-controlled," and to be "pure" (Titus 2:4-5).

The entire family, from children to adults, needs guidance

from the Church for their reading and viewing habits. I've found that using specific illustrations from magazines, novels, programs, and movies stimulates controversial, but usually very healthy, discussion.

We must do more than serve as censors by hitting on the "do nots" of sex. We must build a positive foundation. God's hatred of sexual sin should always be stressed in the light of his zeal to maintain the beauty and purity of marital sex.

We should recommend that our people read Christian books that deal positively with sexual relations in marriage.[4] Otherwise, they will read the bestselling secular books that are usually devoid of moral foundations. Clearly, the people in our churches *will* hear about sex—from everywhere. Why not tell them what *God* says about sex and how they can have their questions answered in appropriate literature that regards marriage and sex as sacred.

The Church needs to develop a climate of openness about sexual struggles. Those who struggle with sexual temptation should feel the same freedom to come for help as those who battle depression or need marriage counseling.

Say It from the Pulpit

Such a climate of openness is not developed merely in the counseling office or small groups but from the pulpit. If those who preach never speak about sex or always speak of sexual sinners with wholesale condemnation—never as candidates for redemption and forgiveness—sexual sin will continue to grow and fester. Like a cancer it may surface in tumors here and there, but a large pocket of malignancy will exist—and breed—beneath the surface.

Sexual sin must be addressed not only directly and openly, but in the context of Christ's offer of forgiveness, cleansing, and a transformed life.

Years ago in our church another pastor and I preached a short sermon series on sexual purity. The response was phenomenal. The number of tapes ordered for each message was more than seven times the average number ordered for any Sunday in the previous six months. I still have six letters I received in the mail and numerous notes dropped in the offering boxes in direct response to this series. When this many people go out of their way to respond to a message, it's because it has touched an area of deep need in their lives. People are eager to hear what God's Word says about sex.

During this series, we also wrote Bible study lessons for discussion in our midweek small groups. Most reported exceptionally rewarding and helpful discussions. The church elders and small group leaders met regularly for their own discussions during the series, and shared honestly their own battles with lust. We were able to encourage and pray for each other—and together commit ourselves to sexual purity.

Biblical Counseling on Sex

Many people will come to the Church for counseling in sexual matters. Whenever the subject is addressed publicly, however, many more will come out of the woodwork. They will acknowledge their sexual struggles and sins and often plead for help. When that happens, the Church must be ready with wise biblical counseling that helps individuals in the nitty gritty of their lives. Premarital counseling should be required and sexual matters should be appropriately dealt with.

Churches can also establish fellowship and therapy groups for those who have suffered traumatic experiences such as abortion and rape. Many churches now have post abortion Bible studies. One church has a thriving ministry to incest victims, many of whom have suffered silently for decades, never having anyone to talk to that they felt could understand. To protect confidentiality, group meetings are not publicly announced, and women seeking to join the group are carefully screened through an application and interview process with a church staff member.

We Need Each Other

John Donne was right. "No man is an island." We desperately need each other's presence, help, and support. Without them, we will never experience what our Father has for us.

Accountability: A Key to Sexual Purity

Accountability boils down to this: I need people to check up on me, to ask how I'm doing spiritually and to tell me when they see weakness or seeds of sin in my life. Nothing is more healthy in the body of Christ than a strong sense of accountability to each other. If I know I must answer to someone, it makes me more conscious and careful to do what is right. Through phone calls, notes, and regular meetings, we need to obey the biblical injunction to "spur one another on toward love and good deeds" (Hebrews 10:24).

Separated from the presence of accountability to his church and family, a college friend told me, "At first I resisted all the temptation everybody had warned me about. But I was so busy in school that I didn't get committed to a spiritual community soon enough. I went to church but didn't really have any other Christian to share with. I began to feel alone, and the things tempting me no longer seemed so bad. Finally, I just wore down and gave in." The result was three years of immorality, a lost witness for Christ, and scars that will remain the rest of his life.

Church leaders are in special need of accountability. Many pastors minister alone. Their position brings unique temptations and attacks from Satan. They need regular accountability to spiritual men in the church fellowship. Even when there is a plurality of pastors, it is easy for the business agenda to overshadow personal interaction at staff meetings. In one church a pastor repeatedly tried to bring up the subject of his personal sexual struggles. But there was never an opportunity; there was always too much business to be done. He finally managed to get the attention of his fellow pastors—*after* he committed adultery.

Other Christian leaders travel a great deal. They fly in and out of cities where they enjoy virtual anonymity. This lends itself to rationalizing: "Who would ever know if I went into this theater or bookstore, or watched this movie in my hotel room, or even if I had a few drinks with the woman I met on the plane?"

These men and women are in great need of accountability to family and friends back home, and to Christians they are ministering to. It is reasonable to help provide accountability during their visit. Regardless of the expense, phone calls to spouse and children are important reminders of true and lasting values in contrast to the devil's tempting lies. Admitting sexual temptation to your wife over the phone gives you her encouragement, prayer, and accountability. (My booklet,

Sexual Temptation, was specifically written to help those in ministry to avoid and resist sexual temptation.)

Prayer is a great way to support each other. But the sad truth is that many of us spend more time praying for our food than for our brothers and sisters. Perhaps many Christian leaders would have turned away from immorality had their people prayed for them. May God teach us what he did Samuel, who said to his brothers, "Far be it from me that I should sin against the LORD by failing to pray for you" (1 Samuel 12:23).

A Climate of Holiness

A spirit of accountability is cultivated in a climate of holiness in which worship is real, Christ is exalted, and lives are transformed. In a climate of holiness, sin is hated—not tolerated, minimized, winked at, ignored, or mildly dismissed (Psalms 45:7; 97:10; 119:104; Proverbs 8:13; 13:5; Romans 12:9). In a climate of holiness the Gospel is seen not as a call to happiness but to holiness. This kind of wholehearted commitment is as contagious in a church as is moral laxity.

The clearest sign of an unholy church (a phrase that is a contradiction in terms) is its high tolerance for sin. The church at Corinth is the primary New Testament example. It was a church full of knowledge and blessed with spiritual gifts, yet riddled with immorality. Paul addressed the issue of immorality in the Corinthian church with the strongest terms imaginable (1 Corinthians 5:1-13). Immorality must be tolerated—though never approved—in the world, but under no circumstances can it be tolerated in the Church. Paul compares immorality and its effects on the Church family to yeast that works its way through the whole batch of dough (1 Corinthians 5:6).

Paul is a realist. He acknowledges that sexual sin occurs in the Church, but he refuses to concede that ongoing immorality is to be tolerated. It must be dealt with directly, decisively, and immediately.

John Stott tells us:

> The Church's witness is impaired by its own low standards. The secular world is almost totally unimpressed by the Church today. There is a widespread departure from Christian moral standards, and unbelievers see no great difference between themselves and Church members. So long as the Church tolerates sin in itself and does not judge itself . . . and fails to manifest visibly the power of Jesus Christ to save from sin, it will never attract the world to Christ.[5]

How Holy Do We Look?

If the Church is to be sexually pure, its members must appear sexually pure. At some point the Church must address the controversial issue of proper clothing. Obviously it was an issue in the New Testament Church since several writers address it.

It has been both ironic and disheartening to counsel men struggling with lust, then attend the church's July 4th picnic and see how some of the women and girls dress. One man told me that every summer is a spiritual low point for him because he is surrounded by women, some of them fine Christians, wearing the latest swimsuits and summer fashions.

Many churches use to sponsor women's aerobics programs that provide excellent opportunities for women to get exercise, fellowship, and bring in non-Christian friends. I greatly appreciated the thoughtfulness of the woman who directed this program in our church. Whenever men were invited, she instructed the women to dress in loose, nonrevealing outfits. (I saw another Christian group in a public place that did not take this care.)

Of course, men as well as women can be caught, innocently or deliberately, in the "let's be sexy" game. Sexiness should be reserved for the marriage bedroom. The Church assembled should be a sanctuary to gain strength to resist the world's temptations, not a factory producing its own temptations. In its services, the Church should be sensitive to modest and pure appearance.

This is a sensitive matter that requires an educational process as well as honest communication. Somehow, though, church members must be taught to give as much attention to preparing their hearts for worship as they do their bodies (1 Peter 3:3-4).

Confronting and Disciplining for Sexual Sin

If the Church is to be a holy community, we must confront each other with the truth. Apathy or permissiveness disguised as love do no one a favor. We must remember that our primary objective is holiness, not happiness. Our goal is not to help each other *feel* good, but to help each other *be* good. Honesty, reproof, and discipline are a painful but essential part of the believing community. Whenever they are absent, immorality and a host of other sins will prevail.

In Ephesians 5:3-13 Paul affirms that the slightest suggestion of immorality is out of place among God's people. They are neither to act out nor even speak of immorality in a flippant, crass, or joking manner. The only justification for speaking of immorality is to expose its sinfulness and bring to bear the light of God's holiness. Part of being accountable in Christ's body is to lovingly confront each other when we speak and joke about what is sexually inappropriate.

Disciplining the Church Leader

Those in positions of leadership are particularly subject to public discipline: "Those, [elders] who sin are to be rebuked publicly, so that the others may take warning" (1 Timothy 5:20). I know of pastors guilty of immorality who have quietly resigned from one church (everyone wanted to avoid a scandal), only to reappear at another church that was totally ignorant of their previous track record. Too often they repeat their sins, largely because they have been protected from sin's full consequences and never been helped to overcome their problem.

Such an attempt to guard a leader's reputation amounts to an irresponsible endorsement of a man whose moral vulnerability should have required his stepping down from ministry, at least for a significant season. The leader, his family, his church, and his Lord's reputation all suffer when sin is covered up. The Church must face the fact that the leader in sexual sin is neither a "one-woman man" nor "above reproach" (1 Timothy 3:2; Titus 1:6-7). He is therefore, for the present, disqualified for church ministry.

We must remind ourselves that lust is a sexual sin as well (Matthew 5:27-28). A leader not guilty of physical immorality is nonetheless unfit for ministry if he has a roving eye or otherwise demonstrates an ongoing lust problem through his gestures, actions, or speech. It should go without saying (but unfortunately doesn't) that a man may express appropriate physical affection—such as a hug or a hand on the shoulder— without being guilty of lust.

Every church leader is human and therefore will experience temptation and at times be guilty of a lustful thought. Provided it is properly dealt with through confession and repentance, it does not disqualify him for ministry. It is the ongoing, persistent problem of lust (not just sexual temptation) that could spell disaster for the man and his ministry if it is not dealt with.

The goal of all Church discipline is always restoration, not reprisal. The man guilty of the ongoing sexual sin addressed in 1 Corinthians 5 *did* repent, and as a result Paul tells the Corinthian church to welcome him back—the purpose of discipline had been fulfilled (2 Corinthians 2:7). If the Church is not to tolerate immorality, even less is it to tolerate those whose teachings promote or justify immorality (Revelation 2:20-23). One of the greatest weaknesses of many denominations is their allowance of those who use their positions of authority to promote an antibiblical morality in seminaries and the Church.

Before the Church can say anything to the world, she who is intended to be the spotless bride of Christ must look to herself. "For it is time for judgment to begin with the family of God" (1 Peter 4:17).

WHAT WE CAN DO IN THE WORLD

Otto Piper levels a strong indictment against this generation of Christians:

Modern Christianity has incurred a grave guilt. Our congregations have failed effectively and articulately to protest against the widespread glorification of sexual sins, and have been guilty of serious negligence by enduring degradation and scorn heaped upon the Christian virtues by the radio, the motion pictures, television, and the press. We have no right to plead excusable weakness. Our toleration is a sinful disdain of the divine insight granted us; and thus we are no less reprehensible than those who commit gross sexual sins. Our indifferent and tolerant frame of mind shows plainly that we do not only consider these portrayals of sexual sin unimportant but that we actually give them our inner approval, or even find them desirable.[6]

SALT AND LIGHT

This is not a time to be silent. It is a time to speak out with wisdom, tact, and compassion, yes, but also with strength and conviction. Otherwise, we will never be what Jesus called us to be:

"You are the salt of the earth. But if the salt loses its saltiness, how can it be made salty again? It is no longer good for anything, except to be thrown out and trampled by men.

"You are the light of the world. A city on a hill cannot be hidden. Neither do people light a lamp and put it under a bowl. Instead they put it on its stand, and it gives light to everyone in the house. In the same way, let your light shine before men, that they may see your good deeds and praise your Father in heaven" (Matthew 5:13-16).

In the sixties and seventies, American evangelicals were confident that Christ would return immediately. There was no need to change society. Only the humanists and liberals were trying to patch up a world we knew was destined for destruction and which we expected to leave soon anyway. We were so busy buying millions of books on the end times and listening to prophecy preachers tell us the details of the Rapture, Tribulation, and Antichrist, our society's problems seemed dull and irrelevant.

In the eighties and nineties it began to sink in with many of us that while Christ will come again, and He can come at any time, He may not choose to come in our lifetime (and there's nothing we can do either to predict or change His timetable). Meanwhile, we have neglected to speak out and become involved in issues that have produced an antimoral and anti-Christian social climate for which we, our children, and our grandchildren will pay dearly.

Many Christians are no longer content to stand idly by while their nation is sucked down a secularist drain they have not even attempted to plug. They have stopped labeling social-ethical issues "hands off." They are no longer content to spend their days blissfully listening to Christian radio, positioned for the Rapture in their favorite recliner.

There is no end to the ways Christians can minister to the spiritual needs of people through addressing the problems created by the sexual revolution.

• We can reach out to the homosexual community, developing relationships with those that are open and making ourselves available in a time of crisis or need.

• We can address the rape problem by working for tougher laws and tougher enforcement.

• We can fight pornography, which feeds rape.

• We can also train or support training to increase mental preparation, self-confidence, and proper response to potential assaults.

A welcome change is taking place—Christians are taking seriously Jesus' call to be salt in a tasteless world and light in the midst of moral darkness.

For example, there is now a network in place throughout the country of some 4,000 pro-life centers that are providing alternatives for women considering abortion. These centers provide a variety of services. They offer free pregnancy tests and counseling. Some provide free medical care, ultrasounds, and some even provide free room and board if necessary. Many of them also give baby food and clothing. Pregnant women are welcome to call 1-800-BETHANY to learn of the center closest to them. In fact, these abortion alternative centers are the largest grassroots movement of assistance to one group of needy people ever offered in American history.

POLITICAL AND SOCIAL INVOLVEMENT

More believers than ever are becoming socially and politically active. There is a great need, through mobilizing, lobbying, and voting, for believers to influence legislation in this country. Stiffer penalties for child pornography, for instance, have arisen only because concerned citizens pushed the issue. They will be enforced only if we continue to push.

We need tougher legislation applying to adult pornography, prostitution, and rape. But legislation is no better than its enforcement. For this reason we need better judges, better lawyers, more policemen, more prison facilities, and reformed jury and parole systems. We need to oppose antifamily and antichurch legislation, for the family and the Church are the moral fiber of the nation.

"But you can't legislate morality." No, but we can have moral legislation that protects the innocent and punishes the guilty. We can't make people behave morally, but we can legislate the consequences when they don't. That is precisely the purpose of laws.

Those Christians in government should be prayed for, helped, and encouraged to make biblical decisions, not politically expedient ones (a Christian politician can vote unbiblically, just as a non-Christian can vote biblically).

There is a desperate need for more Christians in government at the local, state, and national levels. We must not surrender this critical turf to those, both well-meaning and otherwise, living in spiritual and moral darkness. The Church should encourage individual believers to be involved in the social and political arenas, even though the Church itself must be careful not to become a political organization.

Becoming Informed and Involved

Effective community involvement requires a knowledge of the issues, local government structure, and the identity and sphere of influence of local officials.

Knowledge of the issues can come from the media and from personal contact. There is little value in knowing the issues, however, unless we are developing a firm grasp of the relevant biblical principles. Otherwise we will know what to talk about—but not what to say. Churches need to give their people a solid biblical education and an ability to bring Scripture to bear on moral and social issues.

Writing letters and making phone calls to local officials is the most basic means of involvement. Elected officials are particularly sensitive to this input because they are eager to please their constituencies.

When the opportunity arises, Christians can give public testimony at community hearings and forums on significant issues and proposals (e.g., on regulating cable television). A carefully written, concise statement shows deep concern when read at such meetings.

A woman in our church spoke out at a hearing about a proposed ordinance to permit nude dancing in her county. One of the public officials specifically stated it was this woman's testimony that changed her mind—and that official's vote kept the ordinance from passing. Had this Christian woman been too tired or too busy to attend that meeting, one more piece of ground would have been gained by the forces of evil.

The next level of involvement is volunteering time to serve on committees and task forces (e.g., on pornography or teen prostitution). Financial contributions are another significant means of involvement.

One Church's Approach to a Social Problem

The experience of a nearby church provides a good model for social involvement. Prostitutes daily worked the streets outside of this Portland church, their customers sometimes even parking in the church's lot. Thinking their duty was to flush out this vice (which is one step ahead of many churches who would simply ignore the problem), church members took out cameras to scare away business. When that didn't work, they picketed, carrying signs that read "Prostitution is illegal and immoral." That didn't work either. Soon the whole congregation made an antiprostitution march. They only succeeded in pushing the prostitutes further up the block.

When all else failed, one of the pastors took a different approach. He personally passed out business cards to the prostitutes, giving them a number to call if they wanted someone to talk with. When the weather turned cold, he and others took them coffee and doughnuts. At Easter they gave them baskets filled with candy. They even gave them presents on their birthdays.

After a while these young women began to come to the church for help. The pastor and others in the church opened their homes to them. Within two years fifteen women left prostitution, and several of these had come to Christ.

INFLUENCING THE MEDIA

Contacting the sponsors may be the most effective means of improving not only television, but most other media. Television, radio, magazines, newspapers—all are heavily dependent upon their advertisers or sponsors. The sponsors want their name to strike a positive note so that consumers will buy their products. They shun negative publicity.

Suppose ten thousand Christians dropped their subscriptions to *Sports Illustrated* to specifically protest the sexual exploitation of its annual swimsuit issue. Do you think this would leave an impression with the publisher?

You can obtain sponsors' names by checking the products they advertise, and their addresses from their local representatives (listed in the phone book) or *Standard and Poor's Dictionary* found in most libraries. Individuals and churches can help others by bringing sample letters, with current names and addresses, as models for others. The most effective letters are personal, not photocopies, verbatim duplicates or e-mails.

The best long-term means for Christians to influence television and other media is for more to enter the field. If there were more skilled Christian screenwriters, directors, and producers—and actors who would not sell out their principles for "a good part"—the industry could be positively influenced from the inside. Unfortunately, many believers are avoiding these fields because they are becoming corrupt, thereby destining them to further corruption instead of possible reform.

WHAT TO DO ABOUT PORNOGRAPHY

The clearest demonstration of what concerned individuals and communities can do is in the area of pornography. Whole cities have succeeded in banning its sale. They not only have no adult book stores, but their convenience stores do not even carry *Playboy*. They've also blocked efforts toward adult cable TV channels. All because concerned citizens spoke out with one voice.

Many fine antipornography laws exist. The major problem is their lack of enforcement. In a five-year span, one Memphis attorney prosecuted sixty violators of federal pornography laws, and fifty-nine of the sixty were convicted. Yet they were given nine to eighteen months sentences and small fines (relative to their earnings). Most are never prosecuted at all or walk away with no more than a slap on the hand. Whenever there is a strong public outcry against pornography, the legislators and the courts respond. Whenever there isn't, they don't.

Specific Steps to Counter Pornography

When you see objectionable material sold in a store, ask to speak to the manager and courteously share your objections. I have found most managers are genuinely interested and concerned when they receive this kind of input. If the situation hasn't changed after a few weeks, speak to the manager again and tell him you feel so strongly about your objection that you will have to take your business elsewhere—and that you will recommend your friends do the same.

When I saw a store at a nearby family mall with lewd posters in its windows, my first response was to write letters to the store and to the mall owners. I took down the name, but neglected to write. A week later a woman in our home Bible study group said she had also seen the posters and had called the store to protest. When she was told that the posters would stay, she called the central office two thousand miles away. She talked to a company executive who thanked her for her concern and told her he would see to it *immediately* that the manager took the posters down.

Quick and effective results often come from taking the time and trouble to get involved. The key is to be both congenial and firm. You may be amazed at the results. Two large grocery chains in the Pacific Northwest stopped carrying sexually exploitive magazines simply because some people cared enough to speak out.

We must always have a positive attitude, uplifting and commending good literature and programming as much as we attack the bad. While the Church stands against obscene practices and literature, it should be there to provide decent literature and a decent example that teaches a positive view of sex. Our image should not be that of vicious crusaders but of profamily and procommunity servants.

For every stand we take, whether it be antiabortion, antipornography, or antiprostitution, we must provide alternatives. We must not just say, "Get teen prostitutes off the street," but, "We'll open our home to one of them."

A FINAL WORD

Early in the twentieth century, a great spokesman of the biblical faith, G. Campbell Morgan, saw clearly the Church's responsibility to its society:

> The Church is responsible for the religious life of the city, for the moral standards of the city, for the social order of the city.
>
> If you can persuade me that we have no responsibilities, that the Church exists merely for the conserving of the life of her own members, then I will leave the Church, and join with others who have a keener sense of moral and religious responsibility; but it is impossible to persuade me to that conclusion in the light of the New Testament teaching. . . .

The Church is against the city as it is, in order to make the city what it ought to be. The Church lifts her voice in protest against iniquity in the city or nation, because her business is to make the city and the nation what God would have them be.[7]

We cannot minister to those in bondage to spiritual Egypt by making Egypt a better place to live, but by offering a new and different citizenship, a radically different way of life. Our culture doesn't just need cosmetic changes, it needs an exodus from sin and a righteousness that can only be found in Christ. Our community needs not just reform, but redemption; not just renovation, but the Redeemer. We must take a stand for righteousness, yes, but always as a platform to share the one true Source of righteousness—the Lord Jesus Christ.

We must listen once more to Edmund Burke, whose words apply equally to the family, the Church, and the nation:

All that is necessary for the triumph of evil is that good men do nothing.

Chapter 11, Notes

1. In his excellent book, *Growing Up Straight* (Chicago: Moody Press, 1982), Dr. George Rekers develops these and many other important aspects of raising children with proper sexual identities. I highly recommend this book for all, especially parents of young boys.

2. Jeane Weston, *The Coming Parent Revolution* (Chicago: Rand McNally and Co., 1981), 229.

3. Elisabeth Elliot, *Passion and Purity* (Old Tappan, N. J.: Fleming H. Revell Co., 1983), 147.

4. For instance, *The Gift of Sex* by Clifford and Joyce Penner-, Intended for Pleasure by Ed and Gaye Wheat; and *The Act of Marriage* by Tin and Beverly LaHaye.

5. John R. W, Stott, *Confess Your Sins* (Philadelphia: The Westminster Press, 1964), 49.

6. Otto A. Piper, *The Biblical View of Sex and Marriage* (New York: Charles Scribner's Sons, 1960), 200.

7. G. Campbell Morgan, *Living Messages of the Books of the Bible* (Old Tappan, N.J.: Fleming H. Revell Co., 1912), 123-25, 128.

CHAPTER 12

Where Do We Go From Here?

Long ago Alexander Pope described the process of moral desensitization that has come to characterize not only America but the American Church:

> Vice is a monster of such horrid mien,
> That to be hated needs but to be seen;
> But when seen oft, familiar with its face,
> We first endure, then fondle, then embrace.

Sexual immorality is so much a part of our environment that it is becoming no more remarkable than the air we breathe or the ground we walk on. It is rarely startling and seldom hated. Most believers are now enduring it, many fondling it, some embracing it. My prayer is that this book has helped to shake us from complacency and challenged us to take the scriptural steps to change ourselves, our families, our churches, our communities, and our nation—to change while there is still opportunity to change.

There are several kinds of readers I find myself concerned about as this book ends. *First, the one who does not yet know the Lord Jesus Christ.* To him or her I can only say that while the moral life is far superior to the immoral, no efforts toward moral reform can earn us God's favor. We must come to Him on His terms, not ours. He offers love and forgiveness to all who swallow their pride and bend their knee to Christ, who died on a cross for our sins and offers us his own moral purity.

I am equally concerned about the reader, believer or unbeliever, who feels the concerns of this book are much ado about nothing—that sex outside of marriage is really not so bad and sometimes even acceptable, or that there is little or no harm done by an indulgence here, a compromise there, a little peek here, a slight indiscretion there, a bit of flirting here, an offcolor joke there. He buries every twinge of conscience or conviction in a landslide of self-justification and self-deceit. His powers of rationalization are mighty, but they do not change the truth.

There is a way that seems right to a man,
> but in the end it leads to death (Proverbs 14:12).

Then there is the Christian who believes he or she is somehow above all this, that one so spiritual as himself would *never* indulge in sexual compromise like the moral weaklings around him. This Pharisee looks down his nose at sexual sinners and prides himself in his own supposed righteousness.

Pride goes before destruction,
a haughty spirit before a fall (Proverbs 16:18).

Other readers are not prideful but naive. They don't demean or write off sexual sinners, but simply can't imagine they could ever join their ranks. Unaware of their own vulnerability, they are all the more vulnerable. The man who doesn't think he can be robbed leaves cash on his desk and keys in the ignition. He sets himself up as an easy target. "So, if you think you are standing firm, be careful that you don't fall!" (1 Corinthians 10:12).

Still other readers know only too well the tragedy of immorality. Some are now walking in purity, enjoying Christ's forgiveness and moral strength, but others are yet handcuffed by unconfessed sexual sin or suffering under a load of sexual temptation that repeatedly leaves them writhing in failure and guilt. To these brothers and sisters I offer the words of a friend who wrote this song to coincide with a sermon on sexual purity:

Ask the miner underground "How do you feel?"
Trapped by tons of earth and rock, the tunnel home is sealed.
From the darkness the reply, a muffled hopeless shout:
"The walls around caved in on me and there is no way out,
The walls around caved in on me and there is no way out."

Ask the diver in the sea, "How do you feel?"
Hopelessly his feet ensnared in weeds made out of steel.
From the depth, could he reply, would come a frantic shout:
"It seems the more I struggle here the more my
    strength gives out,
It seems the more I struggle here the more my
    strength gives out."

Ask the sad believer, "How do you feel?"
Ruled by passions ill-conceived, lustfully he reels.
And from a mind that's torn in two his heart can
      barely shout:
"God, I hate the trap I'm in, I hope no one finds out,
God, I hate the trap I'm in, I hope no one finds out."

Ask the God who made the man, "How do You feel?"
The Holy God who judges sin, in pain that's unconcealed.
From a heart that breaks with love, He's always crying out:
"Son, you're Mine, your battle's Mine and I have
      heard your shout,
Son, you're Mine, your battle's Mine, please
      let Me help you out!"[1]

Finally, I am concerned for the reader whose faith in Christ and confidence in Scripture has been so undermined, he feels the Church has no definitive answers or clear moral standards to offer a world sick with uncertainty. Whenever Scripture counters the prevailing winds of society (which is almost at every turn), this hapless skeptic-saint finds himself uncomfortable with his faith. He has heard so much about tolerance and pluralism and open-mindedness and political correctness that he is almost embarrassed by Scripture's no-nonsense declaration of right and wrong.

Taking his cue from some Church leaders, he apologizes for, hedges on, and qualifies the Bible's position on sexual morality (and almost every moral issue). In a world offended by certainty, he dodges at all costs the sin of dogmatism and does penance by saying, "Of course, we Christians don't have all the answers."

Harry Blamires responds to this approach:

> Let it be said firmly that the bogus humility represented by the "we haven't got all the answers" line is as far from Christian virtue as lust is from love. Whatever else our Lord was accused of, He was not charged with preserving a sage and mystical silence while the weary, the doubtful, dejected and oppressed threw their tragically unanswered questions at Him. Yet in every other religious journal one picks up today, one reads the amazing sentence, "We must not talk as if we've got all the answers."
>
> Why in God's name not? What is our Christian duty if not to make plain that in the Christian faith the gravest doubts and worries of men are richly answered? What do these prevaricators mean? Have we not got the answers in their eyes? Is our Lord untrustworthy, the Church founded upon an eternal question mark, the faith a fog? It will be time enough to put this slogan on our banner when we have heard a dying martyr proclaim it as the surety of his hope.
>
> The scene is worth picturing. The flames gather around the stake, but the martyr's eyes are ablaze only with faith. "I die gladly. I die at peace with God. My last message to you is this: we must not talk as if we've got all the answers."[2]

The world is looking for answers to spiritual and moral questions. We *do* have the answers revealed to us in God's Word. They are not easy answers, but they are real ones. May God empower his Church not to doubt, hold back, apologize for, or dilute the answers He has given us.

Chapter 12, Notes

1. Paul Thorson, *Trapped*. Used by permission of the author.
2. Harry Blamires, *The Tyranny of Time*.

SELECTED BIBLIOGRAPHY

Davies, Bob and Lori Rentzel. *Coming Out of Homosexuality*. Downers Grove, Ill.: InterVarsity Press, 1994.

Dobson, James. *Preparing for Adolescence*. Ventura, Calif.: Vision House, 1999.

Elliot, Elisabeth. *Passion and Purity*. Old Tappan, NJ: Fleming H. Revell Co., 1996.

Hall, Laurie. *An Affair of the Mind: One Woman's Courageous Battle to Salvage Her Family from the Devastation of Pornography*. Colorado Springs: Focus on the Family, 1996.

Johnson, Lissa Halls. *Just Like Ice Cream*. New York: Bantam Books, Inc., 1995. (Romance novel for junior high/high school girls).

Johnson, Lois Walfrid. *You Are Wonderfully Made*. Minneapolis: Bethany House, 1999.

Laaser, Mark. *Talking to Your Kids About Sex*. Colorado Springs: WaterBrook Press, 1999.

Penner, Clifford and Joyce. *The Gift of Sex.* Waco, Tex.: Word, 1982.

Petersen, J. Allan. *The Myth of Greener Grass.* Wheaton, Ill.: Tyndale House Publishers, 1992. (Deals with adultery).

Roberts, Ted. *Pure Desire.* Ventura, Calif.: Regal Books, 1999. (Deals with overcoming sexual sin and addiction)

Satinover, Jeffrey. *Homosexuality and the Politics of Truth.* Grand Rapids: Baker Book House, 1996.

Smedes, Lewis B. *Sex for Christians.* Grand Rapids: William B. Eerdmans Publishing Co., 1994.

White, John. *Eros Defiled.* Downers Grove, Ill.: InterVarsity Press, 1977. (Psychologist examines the ramifications of sexual sin).

Worthen, Anita and Bob Davies. *Someone I Love Is Gay.* Downers Grove, Ill.: InterVarsity Press, 1996.

RESOURCES AND ORGANIZATIONS

Help for the sex addict or those struggling with sexual sin:

Dr. Mark Laaser
Christian Alliance for Sexual Recovery, Inc.
OASISS OutReach Division
6542 Regency Lane
Eden Prairie, MN 55344
952-903-9209 office
888 HELPHOPE (435-7467)
www.helpandhope.org

www.PureIntimacy.Org
(a division of Focus on the Family
Colorado Springs, CO 80995)

Steve Gallagher
Pure Life Ministries
P.O. Box 421
Dry Ridge, KY 41035
606-824-4444
www.purelifeministries.org

To fight pornography:

American Family Association
(and their affiliates nationwide)
P. O. Drawer 2440
Tupelo, MS 38803
800-326-4543
www.afa.net

Enough is Enough
Monique Nelson
P.O. Box 26228
Santa Ana, CA
92799-6228
www.enough.org

Bill Johnson
American Decency Association
P.O. Box 202
Freemont, MI 49412
231-924-4050
www.americandecency.org

Citizens for Community Values
Phil Burress (former porn addict)
11175 Reading Road
Cincinnati, OH 45241
513-733-5775
www.ccv.org

Concerned Women for America
1015 15th Street NW
Suite 1100
Washington, D.C. 20005
202-488-7000
www.cwfa.org

Family Friendly Libraries
Karen Jo Gounaud
7597 Whisperwood Court
Springfield, VA 22153
703-440-3654
www.fflibraries.org

Family Research Council
Jan LaRue
801 G Street NW
Washington, DC 20001
www.frc.org

National Coalition for the
Protection of Children and Families
Rich Scharz, Barb Steffens
800 Compton Road, Suite 9224
Cincinnati, OH 45231
513-521-6227
www.nationalcoalition.org

Authenticity in Action, Intl.
Gene McConnell
513-931-1816